Flexible Working in Organisations

T0386325

There is growing interest in flexible working, not only as a means to manage labour more efficiently and for greater agility, but also as a response to increasing concerns over well-being, work–life balance and participation in the labour force of those with significant non-work commitments (e.g. parents, carers, older workers). As a result, a comprehensive stream of literature on the benefits and challenges of flexible working has developed and led to a body of evidence on the implementation and outcomes of different forms of flexible working arrangements. This book assesses the current state of this literature as follows:

- Background: the authors review the different definitions that have been proposed, policy developments, availability and uptake.
- Outcomes from flexible working: the main chapters focus on the outcomes for employers (e.g. performance, employee retention, organisational commitment etc.), as well as for individual employees (e.g. well-being, job satisfaction etc.).
- Evaluation of extant knowledge: the authors comment on the existing literature and consider the methodological approaches adopted in the literature.
- Conclusion: suggestions for future research are proposed.

Of interest to students, academics and policy-makers, this book provides an expert overview of the empirical evidence and offers critical commentary on the state of knowledge in the field of flexible working and new forms of work.

Clare Kelliher is Professor of Work and Organisation at Cranfield School of Management, Cranfield University. She has a long-standing interest in flexible working and has published widely in this field, including recent articles in *Human Relations, Human Resource Management* and *Human Resource Management Journal.*

Lilian M. de Menezes is Professor of Decision Sciences, Cass Business School, City, University of London. Her research focuses on management practices, performance, attitudes and markets. Lilian's publications include articles in *Human Relations, Human Resource Management, Industrial Relations* and *Journal of Operations Management.*

State of the Art in Business Research
Edited by Professor Geoffrey Wood

Recent advances in theory, methods and applied knowledge (alongside structural changes in the global economic ecosystem) have presented researchers with challenges in seeking to stay abreast of their fields and navigate new scholarly terrains.

State of the Art in Business Research presents shortform books which provide an expert map to guide readers through new and rapidly evolving areas of research. Each title will provide an overview of the area, a guide to the key literature and theories and time-saving summaries of how theory interacts with practice.

As a collection, these books provide a library of theoretical and conceptual insights, and exposure to novel research tools and applied knowledge, that aid and facilitate in defining the state of the art, as a foundation stone for a new generation of research.

Business Models
A Research Overview
Christian Nielsen, Morten Lund, Marco Montemari,
Francesco Paolone, Maurizio Massaro and John Dumay

Mergers and Acquisitions
A Research Overview
David R. King, Florian Bauer and Svante Schriber

Strategic Human Resource Management
A Research Overview
John Storey, Dave Ulrich and Patrick M. Wright

Flexible Working in Organisations
A Research Overview
Clare Kelliher and Lilian M. de Menezes

For more information about this series, please visit: www.routledge.com/
State-of-the-Art-in-Business-Research/book-series/START

Flexible Working in Organisations
A Research Overview

**Clare Kelliher and
Lilian M. de Menezes**

Routledge
Taylor & Francis Group

LONDON AND NEW YORK

First published 2019 by Routledge

2 Park Square, Milton Park, Abingdon, Oxon OX14 4RN
605 Third Avenue, New York, NY 10017

Routledge is an imprint of the Taylor & Francis Group, an informa business

First issued in paperback 2021

Publisher's Note

The publisher has gone to great lengths to ensure the quality of this reprint
but points out that some imperfections in the original copies may be apparent.

British Library Cataloguing-in-Publication Data
A catalogue record for this book is available from the British Library

Library of Congress Cataloging-in-Publication Data
Names: Kelliher, Clare, 1962– author. | Menezes, Lilian M. de, author.
Title: Flexible working in organisations : a research overview /
    Clare Kelliher and Lilian M. De Menezes.
Description: Abingdon, Oxon ; New York, NY : Routledge, 2019. |
    Series: State of the art in business research
Identifiers: LCCN 2019005174 | ISBN 9780815356325 (hbk) |
    ISBN 9781351128346 (ebk)
Subjects: LCSH: Flexible work arrangements.
Classification: LCC HD5109 .K45 2019 | DDC 331.25/724—dc23
LC record available at https://lccn.loc.gov/2019005174

ISBN: 978-0-8153-5632-5 (hbk)
ISBN: 978-1-03-217815-8 (pbk)
DOI: 10.4324/9781351128346

Typeset in Times New Roman
by Apex CoVantage, LLC

Contents

Figures and table

Figures

Table

1 Introduction and background

This book is about flexible working in contemporary organisations. In the following pages we will examine the background to the recent growth in flexible working; the prevalence of organisational policies offering flexible working arrangements and the extent of uptake by employees; the evidence in relation to outcomes for employers and employees and present an overview of some of the contemporary debates about flexible working, including the different organisational approaches to flexible working (employer- and employee-driven) and the extent to which employer and employee needs can be matched. We will examine the different types of flexible working arrangements according to what is being changed and how the arrangement is established.

Flexible working, in its broadest sense, has become increasingly prevalent in many parts of the world in recent decades. In several economies, flexibility in relation to employment has become a central business discourse and one which is strongly linked to businesses needing to be more competitive and agile in a fast changing world, as well as employers acting more responsibly by recognising the challenges employees face in combining work with their non-work lives and expressing concern for employee well-being. Flexible working may enable organisations to match their need for labour more closely with supply, allow them to be more responsive to changes in their environment, and to attract and retain groups with significant non-work commitments (e.g. parents, carers, older workers) who may not wish to, or be able to, participate in traditional ways and thereby achieve greater diversity in their workforce. Many employers have introduced policies, initially termed 'non-standard' working arrangements,[1] which challenge the traditional model of working (typically full-time, at the workplace, during designated working hours) in relation to the location of work, the timing of work and the amount of work done. Governments, at national and regional levels, and policy-makers have also become increasingly interested in flexible working and the opportunities it offers to employees and employers, the wider economy and ultimately to society.

Perhaps not surprisingly, therefore, flexible working has attracted considerable attention from the academic research community. Research interest in flexible working stems from the late 1970s, when scholars in applied psychology became interested in examining the effect of flexitime on worker performance (Golembiewski, Hilles and Kagno, 1974; Schein, Maurer and Novak, 1977). In 1979, in a *Harvard Business Review* article, Nollen (1979) assessed the empirical evidence from studies of flexitime in US corporations. Although Nollen's assessment highlighted that differences in managers' experiences of flexitime were non-significant, he concluded that, although based on small samples, mostly positive results had been reported and had highlighted positive attitudinal outcomes from workers and their managers that could potentially be of benefit to employing organisations. Since these initial studies, the literature has been extended to include research from different fields, including human resource management and economics and has grown at an increasing pace since the 1990s. There now exists a considerable, multi-disciplinary body of research which has examined the provision and uptake of flexible working,[2] the outcomes for both organisations and for individuals, and the factors that may influence these outcomes. In this book we aim to present an overview of this extensive body of empirical evidence and to reflect on the evolution and current state of knowledge about flexible working arrangements.

This introductory chapter will present a brief background to the development of research on flexible working. First, it will examine the main approaches to flexible working (flexibility *of* and flexibility *for* employees), exploring the motivations behind these different approaches and the contexts in which they have emerged. In addition, the section will distinguish between the types of flexible working arrangements according to what is being changed (timing, location, amount of work) and the way in which it is established (formal or informal). The section will also introduce the contemporary debate in policy and practice circles about trying to match employer and employee needs under the banner of agile working and contrast this debate with wider perceptions of flexibility in workplaces.

Chapter 2 will start with an overview of the changing competitive landscape and the social policy and legislative environments in which the various approaches to flexible working have been introduced in different parts of the world. It will examine the evidence on the prevalence of flexible working policies and the degree of uptake. It will also address the research concerned with identifying drivers of both availability and uptake and identify conditions that may facilitate or impede changes to working arrangements.

Chapter 3 will present a summary of the extant research investigating the outcomes of flexible working arrangements. It will start by providing details of the literature searches carried out. It will then examine the various definitions and measures of flexible working that have been adopted in the literature in more detail. The body of the review presents the evidence on outcomes for employers (e.g. performance, employee retention, organisational commitment etc.) and for employees (e.g. job satisfaction, well-being etc.) and the factors which influence these relationships. It will consider outcomes that may contribute to the 'dual agenda', providing concurrent benefit for employers and employees and potentially to society more generally. In addition, this section will analyse the outcomes from different flexible working arrangements (remote working, flexibility over working time, reduced hours), where the extant literature allows for inferences to be made.

The final chapter will assess and offer some comment on the extant body of knowledge in the field, identifying its limitations and weaknesses. It will evaluate the methodological approaches adopted thus far, their suitability to capture changes in working arrangements and their outcomes. The chapter will conclude by offering suggestions on directions for future research to pursue.

Defining flexibility

Despite its common usage, the term flexibility has been used in a number of different ways. These include flexibility in relation to the labour market, indicating an absence of regulation, organisational flexibility, or adaptability in response to change in the environment and flexibility relating to employment. In this book, flexibility in relation to employment will be our main focus. However, even in this sense, the term flexibility has been used to represent a broad spectrum of working arrangements. At a general level, flexible working practices can be divided according to whether they are employer-driven (primarily concerned with efficiency, productivity, speed of response and competitiveness) or employee-driven in the sense that they are intended to accommodate employees non-work lives and help them achieve a satisfactory work–life balance (Zeytinoglu, Cooke and Mann, 2009). These two forms are sometimes referred to as flexibility *of* and *for* employees (Alis, Karsten and Leopold, 2006). The primary concern of this book is to examine the research relating to flexibility *for* employees; however, in order to place these developments in context, some attention will be given in this section to flexibility *of* employees. In doing so, we demonstrate how in practice some of these working arrangements look broadly similar, thus offering the potential for matching the interests of the employer with those of the employee.

Drivers of flexibility

Changes to working practices, including the growth of flexible working arrangements, have been fuelled by a number of more general economic and societal changes that have been observed in recent decades. These include increased competitive pressures faced by businesses, developments in information and communication technology (ICT), greater global integration and supply chains and changes in the workforce resulting from demographic and attitudinal trends (Kelliher and Richardson, 2012). Greater competitive pressure results in organisations searching for ways to manage labour more efficiently and for means to attract and retain talent. Organisations may also need to develop ways which allow them to become more adaptable and responsive to changes and uncertainty in their business environments, as, for example, by being able to increase and decrease labour use in line with demand via the use of short-term contracts. The recent development of the 'gig economy' is a more extreme example of this, since workers are contracted for a specific 'gig', often through an online platform, rather than for on-going employment. For example, a delivery driver may be offered work to pick up food from a restaurant and deliver it to a customer via an app on their mobile phone. Similarly, the growth in the number of self-employed workers in some countries is in line with this trend and has, in some cases, been bolstered by so-called 'bogus self-employment' (Keizer, 2013), where an employer requires their employees to become independent contractors, to then provide services to their former employer.

A recent report by Eurofound and the International Labour Office (2017) argues that new information and communication technologies have revolutionised everyday work and life, by enabling connectivity at any time and from wherever an internet connection is available, thereby uncoupling work from traditional notions of a workplace. Developments in digitisation and the availability of cloud computing, in particular, have meant that many types of work are no longer tied to a specific location. Workers can quite literally do their work from anywhere, and this has facilitated a higher degree of choice for employees over where and when they work. However, this uncoupling of work from a specific location has also provided employers, looking to reduce accommodation costs, with the opportunity to decrease the amount of workspace they provide. For many organisations, this has entailed removing individually allocated workspace and a move to a 'hot desking' environment, with an added expectation that employees work remotely for a proportion of their working time. The ubiquity of mobile technology and the ability to be constantly connected has also changed expectations about employee availability and speed of response. Thus, technology does not only enable employees to connect to work from remote locations and at non-standard times, but has also fostered an environment where a high degree of connectivity and timely responses are expected by their employer (Barley, Meyerson and Grodal, 2011; Collins and Kolb, 2012; Matusik and Mickel, 2011; Perlow, 2012).

Greater global integration generates the need for communication and co-ordination with colleagues and clients in different time zones and with different work week patterns (e.g. in some Gulf states the weekend falls on Thursday and Friday or Friday and Saturday). This may mean that working hours, or days, have to be adjusted in order to achieve real-time communication. This is likely to be particularly significant for multinational organisations and partners in global supply chains, and consequently where teams are distributed in different regions or time zones (Collins and Kolb, 2012). Greater global integration may also increase competitive pressures, for example, where product manufacture or the delivery of back office services are transferred to low-wage economies, thereby requiring organisations to look for more innovative and efficient use of labour.

Alongside these developments in the business world, there have been more general demographic and societal changes that have precipitated the need for greater flexibility. Chen and Fulmer (2018) argue that changes in workforce demographics have prompted a greater number of employers to offer workplace flexibility to employees. These changes include the greater participation of women in the workforce and the increasing number of dual-earner families, resulting in the need to juggle the demands of home-life with work; older workers transitioning out of the workforce; and employees pursuing other activities, such as education or personal interests alongside work. To be competitive in the labour market, employers have responded by developing policies to help employees balance work and non-work commitments. Increased life expectancy, coupled with declining birth rates, has meant that, in many countries, there is a need to encourage people to continue working for longer. The provision of alternative working arrangements both can encourage people to remain in the workforce for longer (or even re-enter), but may also facilitate participation in work by older members of the population, who are unable to work in traditional ways (Eurofound, 2015; Loretto and Vickerstaff, 2015). For example, home working may allow those who are less mobile and unable to travel to a workplace to continue in employment.

Governments have also actively encouraged greater flexibility both for individuals and in the labour market. Employers have sought to introduce more flexible, and recently termed agile, work practices and have also offered greater choice to employees over their working arrangements. For example, the UK first enacted the so-called 'right to request' flexible working legislation in 2003, allowing parents of young children to request flexible working and extended this to carers in 2007 and parents of older children in 2009 and subsequently to all employees in 2014. Previous policies had specifically addressed work-family issues, for example, a National Care Strategy (1998) to assist working parents and a work–life balance campaign (2000) attempted to persuade employers of the economic benefits of family-friendly policies (Dex and Forth, 2009). Flexible working policies were advocated by government and campaigners as beneficial for parents, children and businesses, and the economic argument presented that such practices enabled organisations 'to retain staff in whom they have invested and on whom they depend' (DTI, 1998, p. 31). More recently, the UK Equalities and Human Rights Commission has advocated that all jobs should be made available on a flexible working basis, in order to increase opportunities for everyone and to give individuals greater choice about the roles they play at work and at home (Equality and Human Rights Commission, 2017). The Australian and New Zealand governments have also enacted similar legislation and the right to work part-time is available to parents, for example, in the Netherlands and in Germany. In the USA, a Presidential Memorandum issued in 2014 provided the right to request flexible working to federal government employees and provided support for flexible working more generally. Elsewhere, in countries including France, flexible working has been supported through company-level agreements, including the well-publicised 'right to switch-off' agreement, where employees in a bank gained the right to switch off work devices, such as phones and tablets, during specified periods of time, and company e-mails were also prohibited at these times (Vargas, 2016).

Flexibility *of* employees

Flexibility of employees, or employer-driven flexibility, is designed to allow organisations to increase efficiency by utilising labour in non-standard ways, which enable them to match supply and demand and be more responsive to changes in their environment (Bryson, 1999). Whilst this form of flexibility is not the primary concern of this book, we briefly introduce it here, not only to distinguish between different sides in the flexibility debate, but also to allow us to explore the potential behind recent initiatives attempting to match employer and employee requirements for flexibility.

Flexibility of employees can be described according to Atkinson's seminal model of the flexible firm (Atkinson, 1985). This model identified a number of different ways in which employers might use labour in pursuit of organisational flexibility. These include numerical, functional, temporal and spatial flexibility. Numerical flexibility refers to managing labour in a way where the numbers of employees and/or the total number of hours worked by employees are adjusted in line with demand. Thus, for example, this might include the use of temporary, part-time and zero-hours contracts allowing employers to tailor their employment levels to business patterns. More contemporary developments such as increased use of self-employed workers (real and bogus) and the development of the gig economy can be seen as extensions of this trend. Functional flexibility is where employers are able to deploy their staff across a range of tasks. This improves efficiency in the management of labour by reducing 'idle time', since when demand for one type of work is low, employees are redeployed to other work where demand is higher. The extent to which employers can gain from this depends on their ability to forecast demand across their activities and the range of skills their employees possess. Kelliher, Gore and Riley (2002) identified both breadth and depth of functional flexibility. Breadth refers to the range of tasks an employee can be deployed to, whereas depth refers to the extent to which they are able to fully take on an additional role, or merely provide assistance. Temporal flexibility relates to the timing of work. Typically, this has been concerned with the use of shifts, but also relates to arrangements such as annual-hours contracts and compressed working time in forms where it is the employer who varies when time is worked. Spatial flexibility refers to flexibility over the location of work. Traditionally, this has been concerned with the employers' ability to deploy employees across different work sites.

Flexibility *for* employees

This form of flexibility is the major concern of this book. Whilst no universally accepted definition of flexible working exists, here we focus on forms of flexibility which enable employees to make changes to the timing, place and amount of work undertaken, in line with their preferences (De Menezes and Kelliher, 2011; Council of Economic Advisers, 2014). This form of flexibility is offered to employees to help them achieve a more satisfactory work–life balance. Although primarily concerned with work–life balance and employee well-being, there is evidence to show that there are also benefits for the employer, for example, in the form of recruitment and retention (Foster Thompson and Aspinwall, 2009, Lewis, Smithson, Cooper and Dyer, 2001); employee attitudes (for a meta-analysis see Butts, Casper and Yang, 2013) and performance (for a review see Dex and Scheibl, 1999). Flexibility over working time can range from formalised flexitime schemes, where the employee can vary start and finish times, but where core hours are required to be worked, to those that allow a higher degree of discretion and may operate either as a regular or ad hoc arrangement. Studies have used the terms such as time flexibility, schedule flexibility and schedule control, but in essence are all concerned with employee discretion over the timing of work. Flexibility over location of work, often referred to as teleworking or remote working, allows the employee some degree of choice over where they work. This may be a regular arrangement, both in relation to the amount of time worked remotely (e.g. two days a week) and the timing of the remote working (every Monday), or arranged on a more ad hoc basis, depending on both the employee's work and non-work activities. Reduced hours, or part-time working, however, where the employee chooses to work less than the normal contracted hours for the job, is normally more regular, since it involves changes to the contract of employment. In essence, the difference between these flexible working practices and those that are employer-driven is that it is the employee, not the employer, who is able to exercise some control over the working arrangement. There has been some debate in the literature concerning the extent to which these working arrangements should be examined separately (as distinct working patterns), or collectively (since they all relate to having discretion over how work is carried out), and we will return to this later in the book.

There have also been attempts to distinguish between changes to working arrangements that have come about through formal and informal mechanisms. It is generally acknowledged that informal flexible working arrangements are more widespread (Healy, 2004; Gregory and Milner, 2009; Kelly and Kalev, 2006; Kossek, Lautsch and Eaton, 2005; Lambert and Waxman, 2005; Troup and Rose, 2012). Informal arrangements are typically agreements made between an individual and their line manager, whereas formal ones are set up through the employer's flexible working policy and are likely to involve documentation of any changes agreed (De Menezes and Kelliher, 2017). It is argued that the outcomes are likely to differ according to how the arrangement is set up – is the employee simply taking advantage of a benefit offered to them by their employer, or are they making an arrangement with their line manager about having their particular needs and preferences accommodated?

It is also reasonable to expect that both usage and outcomes will vary with the type of occupation and working conditions. Concerning the latter, Putnam, Myers and Gailliard (2014) in an overview of extant research in the field, identify three tensions and contradictions in how flexibility initiatives are developed, enacted and responded to. These are variable versus fixed arrangements; supportive versus unsupportive work-climates; and equitable versus inequitable implementation policies.

Finally, in this section, we briefly consider the emerging debate about the potential for bringing employer and employee needs for flexibility together. As observed by Zeytinoglu et al. (2009), the debates about flexibility of and flexibility for employees have largely taken place in isolation, as separate areas of investigation, and well-established literatures exist in each area. Flexibility of employees has been examined as part of the wider debate on the use of contingent labour. This has examined the use of practices designed to achieve numerical and functional flexibility (see for example Pollert, 1991; Beatson, 1995; Casey, Keep and Mayhew, 1999; Bergstrom and Storrie, 2003; Kalleberg, 2003; Kelliher and Riley, 2003; Edwards and

Robinson, 2004; van Velzen and Wilthagen, 2006). For employees the outcomes of these kind of labour-use strategies have generally been observed to be negative, resulting in, for example, job or income insecurity and work intensification (Kalleberg, 2003; Kelliher and Gore, 2006; Rubery, Keizer and Grimshaw, 2016).

Flexibility for employees has mainly been considered in the work–life and diversity areas of scholarship (Lott and Chung, 2016; De Menezes and Wood, 2006; Lewis, Gambles and Rapoport, 2007; Van Dyne, Kossek and Lobel, 2007). In addition to beneficial outcomes and some unanticipated costs for employees (Kelliher and Anderson, 2010), studies have also identified a number of benefits for employers, including increased levels of job satisfaction, organisational commitment and reduced levels of stress (for an overview see De Menezes and Kelliher, 2011), in line with the 'dual agenda' identified by Bailyn (2006). Flexibility of employees is often an operations management concern for pursuing efficiency and agility, whereas flexibility for employees often stems from organisational efforts to increase diversity and to achieve a more competitive position in relation to recruiting and retaining talent. In practice though, some of these working arrangements can appear to be similar. For example, reduced hours, flexitime and compressed working hours might be used to increase organisational flexibility, but might also be offered to employees as flexible working options. Hence, it is conceivable that there is scope, at least under certain organisational conditions, to achieve a desirable match between the needs of the employee and the employer for flexibility. This would go beyond the dual agenda (Bailyn, 2006), where benefit is gained by both employers and employees from the use of flexible working practices, but rather to a situation where mutual flexibility can be achieved. More recently, some governments have been proactive in encouraging employers to consider how employer and employee needs' can be matched. In the Netherlands this has taken the form of 'New Ways of Working' (Peters, Den Dulk and Van Der Lippe, 2009) and in the UK, Agility (Agile Futures Forum, 2013; CIPD, 2014). The Agile Futures Forum, a UK government business-to-business body, was established to examine ways of doing this. It was established in 2013 by the then UK deputy prime minister, involving a group of chief executives and chairmen from large employers. The agility debate in the UK has been concerned with ways in which activities, motivated by different interests, might be brought together and, notably, has been presented under the banner of agility, rather than flexibility. To gain greater labour efficiency and agility, coupled with the longer-term benefits from increased organisational commitment and job satisfaction, would represent a double win and could have a significant impact on management practice.

In the next chapter, we address the availability and uptake of flexible working arrangements, and briefly examine some of the factors which have influenced the development of flexible working in recent times, including developments in social policy at national and regional levels.

Notes

1 Although this term has become less common as these arrangements have become more widespread.
2 A search of the database Business Source Complete for the keyword 'flexible work*' in the period January 2011 to February 2018 identified over 2700 articles related to the topic that were published during the period. These included scholarly articles, dissertations and reports in specialist magazines in business, economics, industrial relations, psychology and management.

2 Availability and uptake of flexible working

In this section we will examine some of the factors which have influenced the development of flexible working in recent times, including developments in social policy at national and regional levels. Following this, we will present data on the provision and uptake of the various types of flexible working in a number of countries and some commentary on what these data tell us about the dissemination of flexible working arrangements. Finally, we present a brief overview of extant research examining the factors that have been found to influence both the provision and uptake of flexible working arrangements.

In several countries the availability of flexible working arrangements to employees is, at least in part, influenced by the existence of legislation and governmental policy at national and/or regional level, giving employees certain rights to change their working arrangements. For example, in the UK and Australia employees have the legal 'right to request' flexible working arrangements, as do federal government employees in the USA. Legislative support in some cases is specific to parents; for example, in Germany and the Netherlands parents have the right to work part-time following child-birth. In other cases, collective agreements between employers, or employers' associations and trade unions, play an important role in providing access to flexible working arrangements (e.g. Norway, Germany, Australia). Where governments have provided legislative support for flexible working arrangements (e.g. the UK and the Netherlands), this has mainly stemmed from a desire to support working parents by enabling them to participate more fully in the workforce. As such, the focus has been on flexible working arrangements that assist employees in combining work with childcare responsibilities, thereby enabling them to participate and remain in paid employment. Furthermore, retaining skilled workers, particularly mothers, in the workplace can contribute to higher female participation in skilled jobs and help address inequalities such as the gender pay gap. More recently, however, there has been growing recognition that employees may wish to balance work commitments with aspects of their lives other than childcare, resulting in wider support for flexible working.

In many countries increasing life expectancy has meant that a growing proportion of the workforce also have eldercare responsibilities (Eurofound, 2014) and balancing work with eldercare may require different changes to working arrangements than those required for childcare (Kelliher, Richardson and Boiarintseva, 2018). Aging populations (workers 55+) comprise 18.6% of the EU labour force (Eurofound, 2018), and together with the challenges of funding longer retirement, this means that in several countries there is a desire on the part of governments to extend working lives beyond traditional retirement age. Greater flexibility in working arrangements (e.g. reduced hours, remote working, flexitime) can be used as a means of persuading older workers to remain in employment for longer (Loretto, Vickerstaff and White, 2005; Vickerstaff, Baldock, Cox and Keen, 2004). Circumstances relating to employee health may also be a reason for seeking flexibility in working arrangements. Changing societal values and attitudes towards work, together with growing concerns for work–life balance and well-being, mean that employees may wish to have working arrangements that allow them to pursue other personal interests, needs or callings, such as further education, hobbies, fitness and leisure, religious or volunteering activities (Casper, Eby, Bordeaux and Lockwood, 2007; Kelliher et al., 2018; Ozbilgin, Beauregard, Tatli and Bell, 2011).

In addition to national governments, regional governments, such as the European Union, have placed increasing emphasis on the quality of work and have taken steps to promote this. The EU's 'More and Better Jobs' programme makes a commitment not only to employment growth, but also to improve the quality of jobs. Whilst what constitutes quality in relation to jobs has provoked some debate (Clark, 2005), allowing employees a degree of choice over their working arrangements and having the ability to achieve an acceptable balance between their work and non-work lives has generally been seen as an important component of job quality in policy discussions (UNECE, 2010; Walqing, 2010). Being able to reconcile work and private life is seen as key to the quality of work and employment in Europe, as identified in the Europe 2020 Strategy (European Commission, 2010). Linked to this, the recent proposal for a new directive on work–life balance for parents and carers, under the European Pillar for Social Rights, aims to improve access to flexible working and increase its take-up (European Commission, 2017/0085 (COD)). The implementation of policies designed to facilitate achieving a satisfactory work–life balance is also seen as an important element in gender equality, by encouraging a more equal distribution of caring responsibilities between men and women and thereby increasing the participation of women in paid work.

In addition, the UK's former Labour Government's Work–life Balance Campaign, launched in 2000, argued that flexible working arrangements can benefit employers by helping them to recruit and retain qualified staff, especially women, who in most societies are still the primary carers in families. The same argument has been used in the USA, with initiatives such as 'When Work Works' and the Families and Work Institute's model of change (Galinsky, Matos and Sakai-O'Neill, 2013). For employers, responding to employee preferences for a better work–life balance by offering flexible work arrangements may be an important way of recruiting and retaining high-calibre staff in a competitive labour market.

There is also evidence that employers believe that the provision of family-friendly policies, including access to flexible working arrangements, is important. For example, according to a Eurofound (2013) survey, of more than 5000 senior executives and human resource managers in France, Germany, Italy, Poland, Sweden and the UK (which together account for 63% of the EU27 population), a large majority of employers reported that family-friendly policies were seen as 'important' or 'fairly important' for their organisation. Nevertheless, some variation in views between countries was found, with more than 85% of managers in the UK and Sweden reporting that they considered family-friendly working important, whereas it was judged to be less important for their organisations by managers in Poland. Managers also recognised the importance of these policies for their employees, with similar patterns between countries. For example, only just over 4% of UK managers did not recognise these practices as either important or fairly important, which may be a reflection of the relatively long-standing 'right to request' flexible working legislation in the UK. In the majority of countries in the study, employers offered a range of policies and arrangements for flexibility over working time (e.g. variations to daily or weekly hours, individually agreed hours and part-time working), although these were less commonly found in Italy and Poland. Whilst the existence of legislation or collective agreements were the most commonly cited reasons for offering family-friendly policies (except for Germany), employers also identified benefits, such as increased job satisfaction, improved productivity and as a means to assist with the recruitment and retention of qualified staff.

It is worth observing that accurate measures on the prevalence of flexible working arrangements are quite hard to establish. Although a number of studies attempt to do this, they often examine different aspects of flexible working and gather data from different respondents (employer and employee), making it difficult to compare and assess findings. Some ask employees whether they work flexibly and others ask employers how many of their employees have flexible working arrangements. Furthermore, some studies have focussed on availability, either asking employers whether they

offer flexible working arrangements to employees and if so what proportion of the workforce are they available to, or asking employees whether
they have access to flexible working arrangements (perceived availability),
irrespective of whether or not they use them. Equally, sometimes the pre-
cise nature of what is being captured may be hard to discern. For example,
a question about the proportion of employees working part-time may not
distinguish between those that work part-time as a result of their choice
and those who are unable to obtain full-time work. Similarly, figures on the
number of remote workers may not distinguish between those who work
remotely by choice and those who do not have access to working space
at their employer's premises. In addition to this variation in what is being
measured, some of the largest and representative/reliable studies, which are
carried out on a regular basis, have relatively long intervals between data
collection points. In a field where policy and practice developments have
moved relatively rapidly, this can create challenges for obtaining up-to-date
data. Comparison of figures between countries is also sometimes hampered
by different approaches to sampling being used. Notwithstanding these limitations, below we report on the prevalence of availability and uptake of flexible working arrangements, including flexibility over working time, work
location and the number of hours worked, drawing mostly on European data.

Although standard working hours remain the dominant working-time
model across most countries, in recent years there have been a number
of developments in Europe concerning the provision of flexible working
arrangements. Employers have increasingly offered employees the opportunity to exercise some discretion over working time via flexitime schemes
(both formal and informal) and working-time accounts where employees are
able to 'bank' any time worked over normal contracted hours and recoup
this time at some point in the future. The European Company Survey 2013,[1]
drawing on more than 30,000 questionnaire-based interviews with managers in a representative national sample of employers in 32 European countries, found that 66% of establishments across Europe offered employees
the possibility to choose the time they start and finish work. This reflected
an overall increase from 55% in the previous survey in 2009, although
decreased availability was recorded in a small number of countries including Bulgaria, Croatia and Poland. The prevalence of flexitime varied significantly between countries however, with it being offered by more than
80% of establishments in Finland, Denmark, Sweden and Austria, but less
than 40% in Croatia, Bulgaria and Cyprus. The results also showed that
flexitime was more commonly offered, to at least some employees, in service industries and by large employers (Eurofound, 2015). In relation to the
type of working time flexibility where employees can accumulate overtime
to be taken off at a later point, 54% reported offering this to all employees,

with a further 15% offering it to some employees, reflecting an increase from approximately 40% in the 2009 survey. As with flexitime, differences existed between countries with more than 90% offering this to some, or all, employees in Finland, Austria and Germany, but less than 35% of establishments in Greece and Cyprus.

Just under 80% of establishments reported that they employed some part-time workers, with most countries reporting an increase in comparison to the 2009 survey. In the Netherlands, sometimes referred to as the European capital of part-time working, 93% of establishments reported having some part-time workers. Austria (90%) and Belgium (87%) also reported a high proportion of establishments with part-time workers, but in Portugal (22%), Croatia (14%) and Cyprus (33%) this was much lower. The use of part-time work was more prevalent in the service sector and with large employers (Eurofound, 2015). However, it is noteworthy that these figures do not distinguish between those who chose to work part-time and those who do so because full-time work is unavailable to them.

Looking at employee census data, Eurostat figures for 2010 show that just under 29% of employees across the EU's 28 countries have a flexible working schedule. Variations between countries are similar to those reported above with the highest proportions in Finland (55%), Norway (51%) and Sweden (43%) and the lowest in Hungary (7%), Croatia (8%) and Bulgaria (9%). In nearly all cases a higher proportion of female workers had a flexible schedule than male workers. It is noteworthy that in most countries, the 2010 figures represented a decline in the number of employees reporting that they had a flexible work schedule in comparison to 2004. Notwithstanding this, it is noteworthy that 36% of UK employees are reported to have a flexible work schedule; however, this is at variance with the Office of National Statistics 2015 data which reports that only 10% of employees have flexible working hours, illustrating the problems associated with comparing figures from different sources.

Data show part-time working to be a common type of flexible working arrangement across Europe, with 20.5% of all workers in the EU labour force working part-time (Eurofound, 2018), but with significant variation between countries. Findings from the EU Labour Force Survey[2] 2015, a large household sample survey (approximately 1.5 million individuals) covering 33 European countries, suggestie that a majority of part-time workers would prefer to work more hours, and this is particularly so for those who work a small number of hours. Notably, although not evident from general figures, part-time work may be carried out in a number of different ways, including prearranged working hours, or as is sometimes more common in lower-paid part-time jobs, the hours worked may not be regular and/or set in advance (Eurofound, 2010).

Figures from the European Working Conditions Survey[3] 2015 (EWCS), drawing on responses from a representative sample of 43,850 workers aged 15 years and over (16 and over in Bulgaria, Norway, Spain and the UK) in 35 European countries, show that about 18% of workers work remotely or telework. As discussed above, these results show significant variation between countries, with more than 30% of workers teleworking in Scandinavian countries and in the Netherlands, but only 10% or fewer in countries such as Hungary, Poland, Greece and Italy. It is noteworthy that flexibility over the location of work can be hard to assess in general terms because of the different forms that it can take. For example, it may include teleworkers who work away from the workplace for all of the time; those who work remotely for part of their working time (on a regular or ad hoc basis); and those often referred to as 'mobile workers' who work in different locations in line with business demands (e.g. home, workplace, client sites, public locations such as coffee shops and while travelling etc.). Findings from the EWCS 2015 found that across Europe 5% of workers were regular teleworkers working from several different locations, 10% occasional teleworkers and only 3% were regular home workers. Given the nature of remote working, it is clearly more applicable in some jobs than in others. Roles that are relatively independent and tasks that involve greater use of ICT are more suitable than those which require presence at a workplace for machine operation (e.g. manufacturing) or personal interaction with customers (e.g. retail, healthcare).

Considering the USA, data collected by the Society for Human Resource Management from 3227 HR professionals, based on a random sample from their membership database, found that 62% of employers reported that they offered some form of remote working (including 23% offering full-time telecommuting) and 57% flexibility over working time (including 29% offering compressed working weeks) (Society for Human Resource Management, 2017). In addition, as Choi (2018) reports, the US federal government, which is the largest single employer in the USA, signed the Telework Enhancement Act in 2010 and since enactment of this law federal workplaces have been significantly transformed, with a continuous growth in the number of federal employees who are eligible to work remotely.

It is noteworthy that some of the differences observed between countries can be attributed to sampling: different cultural traditions and, in particular, how family members act as care givers; patterns of business activity and the make-up of different sectors in the economy; and how the availability of flexible working arrangements affects the participation in the workforce. The social security system in place is also important, for in several countries there has been greater participation of females in the job market and consequently a move away from the traditional male breadwinner model. According to Eurofound (2012), the predominant model in Europe has become the so-called 'modified male breadwinner', where there is a male breadwinner and the female partner participates in the labour market to some degree, and this model is followed by the dual-earner couple model that presumes a more even participation in the workforce.

Factors influencing the provision and uptake of flexible working arrangements

A number of studies have attempted to examine the factors which influence whether flexible working arrangements are made available to employees and whether employees take advantage of them. The evidence points to availability being uneven (Atkinson and Hall, 2009; Baird and Williamson, 2009) and subject to influences at national, organisational and individual levels (Gregory and Milner, 2009). At national levels the existence of legislative support means, at least in theory, that provision is likely to be widespread, as does the presence of collective agreements covering access to flexible working (Eurofound, 2013). However, in practice, this may depend upon whether employees have a right to flexible employment, such as in the Nordic countries, or just a right to request flexible working, such as in the UK and Australia, and also whether this is available to all or only certain groups of employees and whether this entitlement is subject to a qualifying period of service (Donnelly, Proctor-Thomson and Plimmer, 2012). National context was also found to be relevant by Stavrou, Parry and Anderson (2015), with greater availability of flexible working in countries that promote employment protection and collectivism.

At the organisational level certain management practices, such as the use of 'just in time', may hinder employee control over working arrangements (Henly and Lambert, 2009), but offering flexible working arrangements may also be seen as important in retaining skilled workers (Golden, 2008). In a recent review of the literature, Kossek and Lautsch (2018) observe that different occupational groups have different levels of access to flexible working for work–life purposes. In particular, many lower-level workers were found to be unable to access schedule control or choice over work location, which were found to more commonly available to mid- and higher-level workers. Gender, however, seems to be less important. Chung (2018) found no discernible gender differences for access to schedule control once other factors were taken into account, although female-dominated jobs and sectors reduce access for both men and women.

In relation to take-up, even where legislative support exists, employees need to be aware of their rights, and some studies have found low levels of awareness (Donnelly et al., 2012). Furthermore, others have argued that rights may be undermined by increasing workloads, job insecurity and the changing nature of work (Lewis and Den Dulk, 2010). Kossek and Ollier-Malaterre (2012) identified structural work–life support in the form of human resource management practices and cultural work–life support, such as informal social and relational support from supervisors and co-workers, as important. Many studies focus on the central role of the supervisor in uptake (e.g. Hammer, Kossek, Yragui, Bodner and Hanson, 2009; Kossek, Ollier-Malaterre, Lee, Hall and Pichler, 2011; Todd and Binns, 2013), and their role would seem to be especially important where flexible working arrangements are established on an informal basis. Other factors which have been identified as impediments to take-up include, for example, management resistance, lack of IT infrastructure, the nature of work/position, when flexible working is not seen as normal in the organisation, and the business climate (Choi, 2018; Eurofound, 2013; Lautsch, Kossek and Eaton, 2009).

Notes

1 Details can be found at www.eurfound.europa.eu/surveys/european-company-surveys/european-company-survey-2013-methodology.
2 Details can be found at https://ec.europa.eu/eurostat/web/microdata/european-union-labour-force-survey.
3 Details can be found at www.eurofound.europa.eu/surveys/european-working-conditions-surveys/sixth-european-working-conditions-survey-2015/ewcs-2015-methodology.

3 Reviewing the literature on outcomes of flexible working arrangements

A considerable literature has developed in recent decades that examines the outcomes of flexible working arrangements. Our systematic review of this literature, covering material published up until 2010 (De Menezes and Kelliher, 2011), aimed to provide a rigorous assessment of the empirical evidence on flexible working arrangements, including economic, human resource and attitudinal outcomes, in order to assess whether a business case for their implementation could be made. While in the grey, non-academic literature there appeared to be considerable support for a business case for offering flexible working arrangements to employees, the accumulated evidence at this time, taken together, failed to demonstrate an unequivocal link between flexible working and performance outcomes. Our analysis of the literature suggested that the mixed findings reflected differences in the theoretical frameworks, units of analysis, methodologies employed and, most noticeably, definitions and measurements used. Hence, we called for greater clarity in this field of research in order to enable comparability between studies, future reviews and meta-analyses. We argued that it was important for the different perspectives on flexible working (managerial approaches, work–life programmes) and variants in the nature of what is examined (organisational policy, employee perceptions, management practice) to be recognised. In addition, we proposed theoretical models (e.g. based on social or gift exchange theories) which could help in understanding the likely pathways from flexible working arrangements to performance. In line with studies of the chain linking practices to performance that emerged in the human resource management literature at the end of the last decade, which imply that employee outcomes are likely to mediate the link between flexible working practices and performance, we suggested the use of multi-level models in future empirical analysis. These would enable the relationships between practices, employee attitudes and performance to be examined, and also to explore moderators at both individual and organisational levels. In addition, it was proposed that longitudinal studies were needed to infer causality, or to examine the time-lag between the adoption of a flexible working arrangement and outcome(s).

The review

Building on this research, the purpose of this review is to assess the new findings that have been published and how the evidence, from which a business case might be inferred, has evolved since 2011. As in our previous review, flexible working arrangements were defined as working practices that allow employees to vary the amount, timing or location of their work (including reduced load or part-time working, remote working, flexitime and compressed working time). Studies of other family-friendly policies, such as childcare arrangements and subsidies, or of practices that do not imply a regular working arrangement, such as career breaks and sabbaticals, or those on contingent and temporary work are not considered in this review. Outcomes examined include those of an economic, attitudinal and human resource–related nature, at both the individual and group (team, workplace, organisation and country) levels.

Searches were conducted using the Business Source Complete database (EBSCO). This includes the main academic journals in the area and therefore should enable the identification of studies presenting new findings to be added to the material examined in the previous review. However, in contrast to the previous review, searches of the grey literature using Google were not considered. This was in part because of the sheer volume of material (1 million+ results) and the difficulty in generalising from it (Adams, Smart and Huff, 2017), but also because our objective was to identify what was new in relation to the business case for flexible working arrangements. As such, we chose to focus specifically on articles that met the standards required for publication in academic journals. It is noteworthy that EBSCO includes academic proceedings, which enables assessment of work in progress that may not yet be at the standard required for publication in an academic journal, but can be informative in terms of new findings from academic research.

This review focuses on articles published between January 2011 and 30 June 2018. The keywords, flexible work* and (outcome or consequence), returned 105 publications, of which 88 were classified as scholarly peer-reviewed journals. These formed the initial sample of studies to be added to the database that was compiled in our previous review of the literature, which consisted of 141 studies, out of an initial sample of 238 pieces of research dating back to the 1960s. Based on citations of our previous review (De Menezes and Kelliher, 2011) identified by Google Scholar on 30 June 2018, an additional set of 13 publications that addressed outcomes of flexible working arrangements was identified as sources of potential new findings. Consequently, a total of 101 abstracts of recent articles were read, with the objective of identifying new findings or emerging themes concerning the likely outcomes of flexible working arrangements, as defined previously. In cases where the abstract did not specifically report findings, the conclusions of the article were also read in order to assess whether the article could add to this review of the literature. As a result of this process, 51 articles were added to our original sample of 141 studies on outcomes of flexible working arrangements, including 16 recent studies of contingent factors on paths from flexible working arrangement(s) to employee outcomes or performance. The searches undertaken also enabled the identification of 17 articles that focus on potential drivers of flexible working arrangements and 5 articles where flexible working moderates the association(s) between human resource management practices and employee or organisational outcome(s).

As a whole, compared with the information available for our previous review, in recent years there has been an increase in studies that address specific types of flexible working arrangements (e.g. telework, flexitime, part-time) via multi-level and structural equation models, using data from different contexts. Analyses of flexible working arrangements are now global, with some studies examining emerging economies and others taking advantage of the existence of large datasets with samples from different countries (e.g. Eurofound's various workplace surveys). Longitudinal studies remain very rare; there are some multi-sample studies and meta-analyses have become more sophisticated, in the sense that likely moderations are also considered. Most of the evidence from meta-analyses and recent reviews of the literature corroborate our previous findings on the potential benefits to the employee and likely human resource outcomes, but offer a less clear picture on the likelihood of links with economic performance.

A lack of clarity over what is actually meant by the term flexible working arrangement remains an outstanding issue. Table 3.1 gives examples of the different definitions and measures being used in various studies. It can be seen that by the term 'flexible working', studies can mean different things: a range of options to work flexibly, at least one type from a set of options, a policy being available etc. Moreover, even where the working arrangement was clearly framed as an employee- or family-friendly practice, the measure of what constitutes the flexible working arrangement can also vary. For example, in some cases flexible working arrangements were described as an element of a family-friendly approach that was distinct from childcare benefits and care leave, while in others, any practice or policy in the organisation that could reflect a family-friendly

Table 3.1 Concepts, definitions and measures of flexible work arrangements

	Definition	Measure(s)	Examples of references
Generic concepts			
Flexible working	Employee has access to a range of flexible or non-standard work arrangements	Availability of any form (index, aggregate)	Campbell-Clark (2001), Halpern (2005), McCampbell (1996), Nadeem and Metcalf (2007), Shockley and Allen (2007), Chen and Fulmer (2018)
		Percentage of employees in a manager's work unit using one or more type of flexible work arrangements	Pitt-Catsouphes et al. (2015)
		Bundles of non-standard work patterns	Stavrou (2005), Sweet et al. (2017), Berkery, Morley, Tiernan, Purtill and Parry (2017)
		Formal versus informal access	De Menezes and Kelliher (2017), Townsend et al. (2017)
		Requested flexible working	Cooper and Baird (2015), Rose (2017)
Work–life benefit *Family-* *responsive HRM*	Practices that enable employees to better manage the interface between work and family	Flexible work included in a measure of family-friendly policies	Allen (2001), Batt and Valcour (2003), Brough et al. (2005), Butts et al. (2012), Grover and Crocker (1995) Eaton (2003), Hannah (1994), Thompson et al. (1999), Wang and Walumbwa (2007), Wise and Bond (2003), Wood et al. (2003), Wood and de Menezes (2007)

	Employee-perception of support for work–life balance including that they can work flexibly	Forsyth and Polzer-Debruyne (2007), Rothausen (1994), Wang and Walumbwa (2007)
	Flexible work-home arrangements	Sok et al. (2018)
	Formal and informal availability of work-family policies	Eaton (2003)
Regular versus irregular flexibility HRM	Employees can exercise choice on when, where and for how long they engage in work-related tasks	Availability and use of flexibility HRM, where irregular concerns sabbaticals and leaves — Bal et al. (2015), Bal and Dorenbosch (2015)
Career customisation	Employees customise how they work	Whether or not employee has a customised career profile — Bal et al. (2015b), Kelly and Moen (2007)
Flexible workplace practices	Numerical, flexible and functional flexible practices	Flexible working is included in different dimensions in a context of high-performance working systems — Whyman and Perescu (2014), Stirpe and Zárraga-Oberty (2017)
Flexibility	How free is the worker How much control the worker has	Locational flexibility and extent of flexibility Control over different areas of workplace flexibility — Donnelly (2006) Crowley and Kolenikov (2014)

(*Continued*)

Table 3.1 (Continued)

	Definition	Measure(s)	Examples of references
Specific concepts			
Schedule flexibility	Employee is able to exercise some choice over time when Work is carried out	Whether employees decide when to arrive and leave work	Baltes, Briggs, Huff, Wright and Neuman (1999), Christensen and Staines (1990)
		Whether employee reports having flexibility of working hours	Schein et al. (1977), Lyness et al. (2012)
			Costa et al. (2004: Costa, Sartori and Akerstedt, 2006), Golembiewski et al. (1974), Grover and Crocker (1995), Hyland, Rowsome and Rowsome (2005), Kelly et al. (2008), Perry-Smith and Dumas (2007), Scandura and Lankau (1997), Shepard et al. (1996), Thomas and Ganster (1995)
		Before versus after introduction of flexitime	Harrick, Vanek and Michlitsch (1986)
		Introduction of flexitime versus one year later	Dalton and Mesch (1990)
			Krausz and Freibach (1983)
		Introduction of flexitime versus two years later	Johnson et al. (2008), Lapierre and Allen (2006), Orpen (1981), Schein et al. (1977)
		Users versus non-users	
		On flexitime schedule (core + varying hours) versus on fixed schedule	Greene (1984), Kaufeld et al. (2004), Kim and Campagna (1981), Narayanan and Nath (1982), Rainey and Wolf (1981)
		Flexitime versus staggered versus fixed	Harvey and Luthans (1979), Pierce and Newstrom (1982, 1983)

	Formal use	Ronen and Primps (1980)
	Availability and use	Hohl (1996), Hooker, Neathey, Casebourne and Munro (2007)
	Whether employee versus whether management decides	Costa et al. (2006), Peretz, Fried and Levi (2018)
	Scope for control and changes in work hours	Piasna (2018)
	Extent of temporal flexibility	Lehdonvirta (2018)
	Flexibility of daily start/finish times, flexibility of work times over the year, general control over working hours	Bryan and Sevilla (2017)
	Bank time (credit/debit) hours	Christensen and Staines (1990)
	Formal and informal use	Kelliher and Anderson (2008)
	Participation in a telework/telecommuting programme	Bailey and Kurland (2002), Di Martino and Wirth (1990),
	Virtual versus traditional worker	Hill, Ferris and Martinson (2003)
		Hill et al. (1998), Johnson et al. (2008), Kraut (1989), Shamir and Salomon (1985)
Remote working	Employee is able to work away from the workplace	Availability and extent of use of home working	Hohl (1996), Hooker et al. (2007), Meyer, Mukerjee and Sestero (2001)
	Formal and informal use	Kelliher and Anderson (2008), Kossek et al. (2005)
	Use	Lapierre and Allen (2006), Martinez-Sanchez et al. (2007a, 2007b), Moore (2006)

(Continued)

Table 3.1 (Continued)

	Definition	Measure(s)	Examples of references
Specific concepts			
		Able to work from home at least 2 days/week	Madsen (2003)
		Works 3 days/week at home	Frank and Lowe (2003)
		Telework-status	Sungjoo (2018)
		Different implementations of online platform working, home-based jobs	Lehdonvirta (2018)
Compressed working time	Employee works full-time hours in fewer days than is normal for workplace	Time since introduction	Baltes et al. (1999)
		4/40 week versus control (5/40)	Dunham, Pierce and Castañeda (1987), Facer and Wadsworth (2008)
		4/40 week: before and after introduction	Greene (1984)
		Being on compressed work scheme	Hyland et al. (2005), Ronen and Primps (1980)
		3/38 week versus control (5/40)	Latack and Foster (1985)
		3/40 week: before and after introduction	Vega and Gilbert (1997)
		Compressed versus non-compressed (before and after)	Venne (1997)
		Availability and extent of use	Hohl (1996)
Reduced hours	Employee is able to reduce hours worked	Use	Branine (2003), Kossek and Lee (2008), Meyer et al. (2001)
		Formal use by choice	Hill et al. (2006)
		Availability and use	Hohl (1996), Hooker et al. (2007)
		20% reduced load	Rogier and Pagett (2004)

approach were included in the measure of family-friendliness, meaning that flexible working arrangements were bundled with childcare and other practices that were targeted at parents. Furthermore, some authors differentiated between regular and irregular flexible working arrangements, while others discriminated between formal and informal arrangements, the amount of actual choice available to the employee or the degree to which the arrangement could be customised. Similar variations in measures and definitions were also observed with respect to types of flexible working arrangements, as shown in the second part of the table, and are consistent with observations from a recent review of the literature that was restricted to examining telecommuting (Allen, Golden and Shockley, 2015). In summary, taking into account the variance in what has been measured in the literature, there is a need to be careful in interpreting and making generalisations from findings.

It is noteworthy that the research in relation to flexible working has emerged in a number of identifiable phases. Figure 3.1 illustrates the evolution of this research. Early interest in the 1970s was concerned with attempting to assess the impact of flexitime on worker performance. From the late 1980s onwards studies began to focus on remote working when developments in information technology enabled greater working away from the workplace. The late 1990s and the 2000s saw interest emerging in the use of 'family-friendly practices' addressing the provision of flexible working arrangements as part of programmes designed to assist employees achieve a better work–life balance. More recently we have seen a concern to evaluate the extant evidence, with a number of literature reviews and meta-analyses being published, along with greater examination of factors mediating the relationship between flexible working arrangements and performance-related outcomes.

In the next sections an overview of the accumulated body of evidence on the likely outcomes from the offering and uptake of flexible working arrangements will be presented. In reporting the findings, we consider a causal chain from management practices to performance, as represented in several recent studies of the management practice performance nexus (e.g. Wood, Van Veldhoven, Croon and de Menezes, 2012). As shown in Figure 3.2, such a causal chain implies both direct and indirect effects from flexible working arrangements, as defined previously. In addition, indirect effects are likely to be via employee attitudes (e.g. job satisfaction, organisational commitment), because employees are likely to respond to the opportunity to exercise choice over their working arrangements, and this response may impact their performance via spillover effects at aggregate levels. First, we report the evidence on direct links with various measures of performance.

1970
Golembiewski et al. (1974)
Harvey & Luthans (1979)
Nollen (1979)

1980
Kim & Campagna (1981)
Orpen (1981)
Rainey & Wolf (1981)
Pierce & Newstrom (1983)
Krausz & Freibach (1983)
Latack & Foster (1985)
Shamir & Salomon (1985)
Harrick et al. (1986)
Dunham et al. (1987)
Burke (1988)
Shinn et al. (1989)

1990
Dalton & Mesch (1990)
Di Martino & Wirth (1990)
Grover & Crocker (1995)
Thomas & Ganster (1995)
Boles & Babin (1996)
Shepard et al. (1996)
Glass & Riley (1998)
Hill et al. (1998)
Baltes et al. (1999)
Dex & Scheibl (1999)
Kossek & Ozeki (1999)
Kurland & Bailey (1999)
Thompson et al. (1999)

2000
Bailey & Kurland (2002)
Glass & Finley (2002)
Batt & Valcour (2003)
Eaton (2003)
Wood et al. (2003)
Lapierre & Allen (2006)
Golden (2007)
Van Dyne et al. (2007)

2010
De Menezes & Kelliher (2011)
Butts et al. (2012)
Donnelly et al. (2012)
Martin & MacDonnell (2012)
Allen et al. (2013)
Allen et al. (2015)
Kroll et al. (2017)
Chen & Fulmer (2018)
Kossek & Lautsch (2018)

Figure 3.1 Evolution of the academic research on flexible working arrangements and performance-related outcomes

Flexible Working Arrangements and Performance

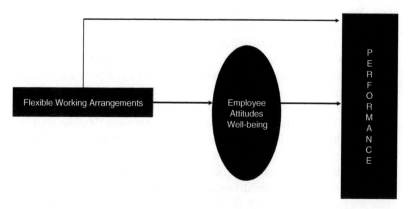

Figure 3.2 Pathways from flexible working arrangements to performance

Direct association with performance

Although there has been considerable interest in the relationship between flexible working arrangements and organisational performance, to date the evidence has largely failed to demonstrate a well-supported and generalisable relationship. Findings from our previous review of the literature on the link with performance varied significantly. Most studies were concerned with productivity and efficiency, and evidence was reported of positive associations with the ability to work flexibly (e.g. Harvey and Luthans, 1979; Hill, Ferris and Martinson, 2003; Kim and Campagna, 1981; Kossek and Lee, 2008; McCampbell, 1996; Nollen, 1981). However, there were also indications of negative associations between flexible working arrangements and performance. For example Meyer, Mukerjee and Sestero (2001) reported a decrease in productivity from job sharing; Rainey and Wolf (1981) showed that there were negative effects on performance from flexitime; and Venne (1997) associated an increase in absence with compressed week working. The majority of analyses, however, appeared to highlight no direct association or negligible effects from flexible working arrangements on performance (e.g. Dunham, Pierce and Castaneda, 1987; Hyland, Rowsome and Rowsome, 2005; Kossek et al., 2005; Meyer et al., 2001; Narayanan and Nath, 1982; Orpen, 1981; Schein, Maurer and Novak, 1977; Wood and de Menezes, 2007). The findings most supportive of a business case related to teleworking found an association with reduced costs or better performance (Dalton and Mesch, 1990; Di Martino and Wirth, 1990; Skyrme,

1994; Kurkland and Bailey, 1999; Stavrou, 2005; Martinez-Sanchez, Perez-Perez, Luis-Carnicer and Vela-Jimenez, 2007a; Martinez-Sanchez, Perez-Perez, Luis-Carnicer and Vela-Jimenez, 2007b), including office and relocation costs. Nevertheless, Bailey and Kurland's (2002) review of 80 academic studies on telework noted an over-reliance on self-report measures, which could have led to bias in the direction of a positive association with productivity. With regards to flexitime, although some of the initial work was very positive and highlighted productivity gains (e.g. Ronen and Primps, 1980; Ronen, 1984), other studies found no association with performance (e.g. Greene, 1984), or reported some negative effects of flexitime (Rainey and Wolf, 1981). Meta-analyses of the link between flexible working arrangements and performance, which at the time covered up to 67 studies, tended to confirm the mixed results in our review. Furthermore, these meta-analytical studies also highlighted the differences in perspectives and research designs in the literature, which meant that many studies were excluded from the meta-analysis. There were, however, some consistencies in the findings, in particular that most of the evidence supported a negative correlation with absenteeism and labour turnover. Gajendran and Harrison's (2007) meta-analysis concluded that teleworking was linked to lower turnover intent. In addition, there have been estimates of reduced absenteeism resulting from flexible working arrangements, varying from around 5% (Kopleman, 1985) to 30% (Bailyn, Fletcher and Kolb, 1997); it should be noted, however, that such estimates were based on relatively small samples, or data from a single department in an organisation.

While analysing the direct association with performance, it is noticeable that most studies rely on self-reported/subjective measures of organisational and individual performance. In addition, cross-sectional data are prevalent and most analyses do not control for when flexible working started, or for other interventions in work organisation that could impact the association with performance. Furthermore, as Kröll, Doebler and Nüesch (2017) report from a potential sample of 3208 studies, their meta-analysis was reduced to include only 28 studies, which included the relevant information on implementation of flexible working arrangements, and within this subset only a very small fraction reported performance data. Notwithstanding these limitations, we now consider the most recent evidence on a direct association with performance.

Allen et al. (2015) conducted a review of the literature on telecommuting, which they broadly defined as a practice that involves utilising technology to work away from a central workplace location. According to this definition, they identified the following related terms in the literature: distributed work, flexible work arrangements, remote work, telework and virtual teams, and also reported the alternative definitions that had been provided in other studies. The authors concluded that 'telecommuting practices may involve some degree of scheduling flexibility, wherein the tasks completed at home vary in schedule from day to day, or are partially carried out during what are considered nonstandard work hours in the telecommuter's work organization (e.g. in the evening)' (Allen et al., 2015, p. 44). This conclusion is in line with Martin and MacDonnell's (2012) meta-analysis of 22 out of 991 studies of telework which, based on different correlation estimates, concluded that telework is positively associated with productivity and workforce retention. Allen et al. (2015), however, adopted a qualitative approach to assess the evidence on the effectiveness of telecommuting practices and clustered the literature according to the outcomes of the studies. While examining performance, they noted that most studies relied on supervisor-rated performance or self-reported measures, and that estimated correlations with working arrangement were generally low. It is thus likely that inflated self-reports of performance deflate the estimated correlation coefficient. According to the authors, there is lack of quantitative evidence at the individual level concerning the link between telecommuting and turnover, but based on quasi-experimental research on a concept that involves elements of telecommuting (Moen, Kelly and Hill, 2011), they argued that turnover can be reduced when employees are given greater flexibility over their work.

In contrast to the previous literature, Allen et al. (2015) included innovation as a likely outcome of flexible working arrangements which, however, could suffer unintended consequences from telecommuting. They noted that Google and other innovative companies discourage telecommuting since they want to foster co-worker interaction and creativity. They also cited research on knowledge sharing and, in particular, findings that emphasise the importance of face-to-face contact in the initial stages of new product development, and evidence that virtual teams wholly working remotely underperformed when compared to other teams. Recent reports of a negative impact of flexible working on team collaboration (Thorgeirsdottir and Kelliher, 2017) also support a likely negative correlation between the uptake of flexible working arrangements and innovation. Nonetheless, as Allen et al. (2015) argued, those individuals who prefer to work from home may also prefer to work alone, and consequently the effects of location flexibility on individual performance are likely to be more complex and contingent on individual characteristics and circumstances. In short, more studies on the link with innovation and creativity are needed, and the future research agenda should also include the likely effects of individual characteristics.

Berkery, Morley, Tiernan, Purtill and Parry (2017) examined the uptake of several flexible working arrangements in 1064 organisations in seven EU countries (France, Germany, Hungary, Ireland, Italy, Sweden and the UK), using the 2008–10 round of the CRANET survey. They identified four bundles of practices, of which one could be classified as employee-focussed.

This bundle was characterised by a high uptake of flexitime (>50%) and a low level of uptake in weekend work, overtime, part-time working, temporary/casual contracts and fixed-term contracts (1–10%). This employee-focussed flexible working cluster was found to have significantly stronger association with above-average productivity and lower labour turnover when compared to the other clusters, but not lower absenteeism. Overall, their results suggest a positive association between employee-driven flexible working arrangements and performance. Moreover, they also highlighted that when employees work flexibly, they may not attach so much importance to face-to-face contact, and that a higher uptake of flexible working can also be an indication of trust between employee and line manager. In this respect, their findings appear to be in line with German terminology for employee-driven flexible working ('Vertrauensarbeitszeit'), which literally implies trust (Vertrauen) as a main component in any flexible working arrangement.

Along related lines, Godart, Görg and Hanley (2017) specifically examined the relationship between trust-based work contracts and innovation at firm level. They focussed on two arrangements: flexitime, where the employer only gave up a limited amount of control, allowing employees to determine their daily starting and finishing times; and working-time accounts, a credit/debit time accounting system in which overtime (or 'undertime') is carried over as a credit (debit) balance, with the time account needing to be balanced over a predetermined period of time. Their innovation measures were assessed one year ahead (t + 1), the first captured whether an establishment improved or further developed one of their products or services, and the second captured whether the firm improved its production technology or introduced a production technology that was new to the firm. Their inferences, based on a large database that included 16,000 plants in Germany from 2007 to 2011, showed that firms that adopted the two types of flexible working arrangements tended to report innovative activity in terms of product or process innovation. These results were found to hold even when the two types of arrangements were combined. As a result, the authors concluded that the positive association with innovation stems from the amount of control and self-management over working days that is transferred to employees.

Peretz, Fried and Levi (2018) developed a multi-level analysis of data from 4790 organisations in 21 countries extracted from the 2009 to 2010 CRANET survey, including companies that reported data on flexible working arrangements (flexitime, job sharing, compressed work week and telework), cultural practices (GLOBE national values) and had at least 80% of their workforce classified as full-time. They observed that national cultural values and organisational characteristics were related to performance outcomes, via the use of flexible working arrangements. In addition, the use of flexible working arrangements reduced absenteeism and turnover, but this reduction was weakened when the flexible working arrangements were not consistent with the local cultural values. The authors concluded that a misfit between national culture and flexible working arrangements could reduce uptake of flexible working by employees and consequently increase the likelihood of absenteeism and turnover. Their conclusions may explain some of the mixed findings concerning both turnover and turnover intentions that have been observed in recent studies, as, for example, Choi's (2018) analysis of 376,577 teleworkers in US federal agencies, which concluded that employees who teleworked had higher turnover intentions, or de Sivatte and Guadamillas's (2013) study that observed no association between flexible working arrangements (temporal or location flexibility) and turnover intent.

Pitt-Catsouphes, James, McNamara and Cahill (2015) examined the impact of manager attitude to flexible working arrangements on team performance by considering whether a manager's early adoption of flexible working arrangements facilitated team performance. Five aspects of work unit performance were addressed, namely quality of work, quantity of work, completion of work on time, quick response to problems and overall group performance. Based on data from 322 managers and units from a large regional healthcare organisation in the USA from September 2012 to January 2014, they concluded that managers' early adoption of flexible working arrangements was associated with perceptions of greater performance from flexible workers. Their findings may be linked to our own findings (de Menezes and Kelliher, 2017) from a comparison of performance ratings of flexible workers whose arrangements had been set up on a formal basis through the organisation's policy with those that had been arranged informally with the line manager. Based on data from 2617 employees in four large organisations with well-established flexible working, who were mostly professionals, we observed that those who had formal arrangements received lower performance ratings.

Taken together, the evidence on direct performance outcomes from flexible working arrangements suggest a picture where indirect effects via employee outcomes and contingent effects of contextual variables may have a greater role in developing a business case for flexible working arrangements. In the next sections, we focus on employee outcomes and what we have learnt so far from different multivariate studies.

Indirect association with performance

Job satisfaction

In our previous review of the literature, we observed that meta-analyses (e.g. Baltes, Briggs, Huff, Wright and Neuman, 1999; Gajendran and Harrison, 2007; Kossek and Ozeki, 1999) and literature reviews (e.g. Golembiewski and Proehl, 1978; Dex and Scheibl, 1999; Glass and Finley, 2002) indicated positive association between flexible working arrangements and employee outcomes. Job satisfaction, in particular, had been the subject of many studies and the general evidence was supportive of a link with both flexible working and performance. A number of studies compared the job satisfaction of flexible workers and those on standard working arrangements, and on the whole found higher levels of satisfaction amongst those working flexibly (e.g. Almer and Kaplan, 2002; Hooker, Neathey, Casebourne and Munro, 2007; Cranfield School of Management, 2008). Importantly, there was also support for a positive association between job satisfaction and perceived availability of flexible working arrangements, regardless of whether or not flexible working arrangements were actually being used by the employee (Scandura and Lankau, 1997). In other studies, availability or perceived availability alone was only found to have a minor effect, but where these contributed to a view of the organisation as being family-supportive there was a positive correlation with job satisfaction (Allen, 2001; Forsyth and Polzer-Debruyne, 2007).

Some studies focussed on particular types of flexible working arrangements. In relation to remote working or telework, earlier studies found little evidence of a relationship with job satisfaction (Harrick, Yanek, and Michlitsch, 1986; Bailey and Kurland, 2002). However, a later meta-analysis using a more rigorous methodology found a positive relationship between telework and job satisfaction and identified perceived autonomy, gender and experience of teleworking to be mediators of this link (Gajendran and Harrison, 2007). In addition, several studies that examined schedule flexibility also supported a positive association with job satisfaction (Harvey and Luthans, 1979; Nollen, 1981; Orpen, 1981; Hohl, 1996), although others found no association (e.g. Pierce and Newstrom, 1983).

Since 2011, there have been a number of articles published concerned with the relationship between flexible working arrangements and job satisfaction. Examining these in more detail and comparing their findings with previous studies, we judged that a further five articles had something new and important to add to the state of knowledge. A recent meta-analysis on the outcomes of flexible working arrangements and stress management training that included 43 primary studies (28 of which that addressed flexible working arrangements) and covering more than 22,000 employees (Kröll et al., 2017) found a positive association with job satisfaction, specifically flexitime and telecommuting. However, their examination of several potential moderators of this link (age, gender, duration and intention of flexible working intervention) showed no support for moderations.

The work of Masuda et al. (2012) extended the analysis of the potential effects of flexible working by considering country and cultural dimensions.

They examined four types of flexible working arrangements – flexitime, compressed hours, telecommuting and reduced hours – working in relation to a number of outcome variables, in a sample of managers from 15 countries. Based on Cammann, Fichman, Jenkins and Klesh's (1979) three-item sub-scale from the Michigan Organizational Assessment questionnaire, their findings showed differences between country clusters. For managers in their Anglo cluster (Australia, Canada, New Zealand, the USA and the UK), flexitime was the only flexible working arrangement that had a significant positive relationship with job satisfaction, while in the Asian (Hong Kong, Korea, Japan, China and Taiwan) and Latin American (Argentina, Chile, Bolivia, Puerto Rico and Peru) clusters, this correlation was not observed. The authors concluded that the differences were due to cultural factors, such as perceptions of gender or the individualism-collectivism dimension, which relates to the extent that individuals prioritise their own goals over collective goals and, in turn, to how they prioritise family and social relationships. Yet, they also argued that, given other observed differences between Latin American and Asian managers with respect to individualism-collectivism, other cultural dimensions might also affect the association between flexible working and job satisfaction and even managers' perceptions of flexible working.

De Menezes and Kelliher (2017) nuanced the examination of the relationship with job satisfaction further, by examining differences between flexible working arrangements made via formal processes and those that were made informally through an agreement between the employee and their line manager. Based on survey data from four large organisations with well-established flexible working policies, structural equation models showed that formal arrangements for flexibility over working hours were a greater source of job satisfaction, but for remote working it was having informal flexible working arrangements that was positively associated with job satisfaction (and thereby indirectly linked to performance).

Chen and Fulmer (2018) examined the relationship between the number of flexible working arrangements employees perceived to be available to them and job satisfaction using data from the 2011 Workplace Employment Relations Study (WERS). They found that the perceived availability of schedule flexibility was more positively related to job satisfaction than flexibility over location or number of hours worked. In addition, interestingly their results showed that job satisfaction was greater for those who perceived flexible working arrangements to be available to them, but who did not use them, than for those who did. Based on the same dataset and using the umbrella construct of 'work-nonwork supports', Wood, Daniels and Ogbonnaya (2018) considered the association between the use of several flexible working arrangements (including schedule flexibility, home working, job sharing, reduced hours, compressed working time) and well-being-related outcomes (including job satisfaction) and further examined the roles of job control and supportive supervision in this relationship. Their findings showed that the use of these arrangements was indirectly related to well-being outcomes, through job control and supportive supervision.

Finally, Possenriede, Hassink and Plantenga (2016), drawing on Dutch household panel data, examined the correlation between temporal and location flexibility (flexitime and telework) with job satisfaction. They concluded that there were positive effects on job satisfaction. However, there was no evidence supportive of positive effects on labour supply, thus the likelihood of having temporal or location flexibility did not drive recruitment, despite making employees happier.

Overall, and in line with our previous review, the evidence points to a link with job satisfaction, which may be explained by the autonomy afforded to employees. However, the findings in relation to perceived availability and informal arrangements might suggest that being able to work flexibly is also perceived as support and may be indicative of what are seen as more collaborative working relations.

Organisational commitment

In our earlier review, we noted that most studies that had examined the relationship between the provision of flexible working arrangements, designed to assist employees achieving a better work–life balance and levels of organisational commitment, had found a positive association between the two, although some studies had not found any relationship (e.g. Eaton, 2003; Wang and Walumbwa, 2007). Research until 2011 had largely focussed on examining this relationship specifically in relation to schedule flexibility. A number of studies showed that those who were able to exercise flexibility over their working schedules reported higher levels of organisational commitment than those who had a fixed working schedule (Pierce and Newstrom, 1980; Pierce and Newstrom, 1982; Chow and Keng-Howe, 2006). Glass and Finley (2002) reviewed the evidence on flexible working arrangements, including only those studies that they deemed to be strong scholarly studies. Amongst other 'family responsive employment practices', they examined relationships between schedule flexibility, remote working and a number of organisational and individual outcomes and concluded that the evidence did suggest a positive impact of schedule flexibility on organisational commitment. Other studies examining perceived availability of schedule flexibility, rather than the actual use of it, supported a positive correlation with organisational commitment (e.g. Scandura and Lankau, 1997; Eaton, 2003). This might suggest that in an organisational climate that is supportive of flexible working and where opportunities to work flexibly are widely known, positive feelings towards employers are engendered, even if employees do not currently take advantage of these opportunities. Furthermore, research on potential contingent factors, such as the employee's preference for integration or segmentation between their work and home spheres, found that this preference moderated the relationship between flexible working arrangements and organisational commitment (e.g. Rothbard, Phillips and Dumas, 2005). In a related vein, some studies focussed on the association with employee engagement and found a positive correlation between episodic temporal flexibility and engagement, but not when flexibility was regular (Perry-Smith and Dumas, 2007). Taken together, the evidence from our previous review in support of a link between flexible working arrangements and organisational commitment was greater than for other employee outcomes examined and for performance.

Since our earlier review, there has been on-going research interest in the relationship between flexible working practices and organisational commitment. Although schedule flexibility has remained the focus of several studies, studies have tended to examine different types of flexible working. For example, taking a general approach to flexibility, De Sivatte and Guadamillas (2013) examined employee perceptions of the availability of various flexible working options, organisational commitment and turnover intention, drawing on survey data collected from five companies in Spain. Their findings showed enhanced levels of organisational commitment where employees perceived that flexible working was available to them, but found no effect on turnover intentions. Moreover, their results imply that a favourable work-family culture and managerial support are likely to moderate associations between the perceived ability to work flexibly and both organisational commitment and turnover intentions.

More specifically, Lyness, Gornick, Stone and Grotto (2012) examined the relationship between schedule flexibility and organisational commitment, drawing on a large sample of survey responses from 21 countries. They found that schedule control was related to organisational commitment in all countries studied and that this was independent of the gender of the respondent. On a related note, Masuda et al. (2012) examined the relationship between the availability of flexible working arrangements and turnover intentions in country clusters that differed along Hofstede's (2001) individual-collectivism (I-C) dimension. Importantly, their study revealed significant differences between Anglo, Latin American and East Asian countries. They observed that for managers in the Anglo cluster of countries, schedule flexibility was the only type of flexible working arrangement that was related to favourable employee outcomes and that those who had schedule control were less likely to report turnover intentions that can be related to continuance commitment. In the case of Latin American managers, part-time working was negatively associated with turnover intentions.

Martin and MacDonnell (2012), focussing on telework, conducted a meta-analysis on a number of outcomes, including organisational commitment, which they concluded were positively related to telework. In Choi's (2018) recent study focussing on telework, whilst teleworkers reported higher turnover intentions than those in traditional working arrangements and respondents who chose not to telework had the lowest turnover intentions, those who were unable to telework because of barriers (including manager resistance, lack of IT infrastructure, nature of work etc.) expressed the highest level of turnover intention.

Ross and Ali (2017) examined the relationship between flexible working arrangements, specifically flexitime and remote working, on both normative (commitment as a duty/doing the right thing) and continuance commitment to employing organisations. Their results, based on a sample of ICT workers in Australia, showed that access to flexible working practices was an antecedent of normative, but not continuance, commitment. They conjectured that workers with flexible working arrangements feel a moral duty, or indebtedness, to their employer. Furthermore, drawing on the findings from the qualitative stage of their research, they suggested that greater feelings of trust between the two parties are established where an employer allows employees to work in different locations and at different times.

De Menezes and Kelliher (2017) also examined the relationship between flexibility over working hours and remote working with organisational commitment and further distinguished between whether the flexible work arrangement was made formally through the organisation's flexible working policy or was an informal arrangement between the employee and his or her line manager. Their findings showed a positive relationship between informal flexible working and organisational commitment and this was supported when flexibility over working hours and remote working were examined separately. With formal arrangements, similar results were found in each case, with organisational commitment being associated with flexible working arrangements. In a related vein, Bal and De Lange's (2015) study of white-collar employees in seven multinational organisations in seven countries found that work engagement (using the UWES measure) mediated the relationship between a broad view of flexibility, or what they term 'flexibility HRM', and perceived job performance and found some support for a moderating role of age in this association.

As above, Chen and Fulmer (2018) also examined the relationship between the number of flexible working arrangements employees perceived to be available to them and organisational commitment, using data from the 2011 Workplace Employment Relations Study (WERS). In relation to organisational commitment, flexibility over time and place did not show significant differences, but were both stronger predictors than flexibility over the number of hours worked. Similar to job satisfaction, their results showed that organisational commitment was greater for those who perceived flexible working arrangements to be available to them, but who did not use them, than for those who did.

In summary, along similar lines to our earlier review, the more recent evidence reinforces support for a link between flexible working arrangements and organisational commitment. Importantly, this has been consistent even where a greater range of flexible working arrangements have been examined and they have been established via different means.

Well-being

In our previous review, we examined the evidence concerning the link between flexible working and various well-being outcomes, including stress, role conflict (mainly work-to-family conflict), work–life balance and psychological and physical health outcomes. A number of studies had examined the association between sources of stress, arising from individuals fulfilling more than one role (work and non-work roles such as family member) and flexible working. For example, Almer and Kaplan (2002) found role conflict and levels of emotional exhaustion to be lower for flexible workers. Other studies concluded that flexible working plays an important role in reducing stress and improving well-being, for example, a negative correlation between the number of flexible working arrangements available and stress symptoms has been reported (Halpern, 2005). Notably, similar observations have been made with respect to the perceived availability of flexible working policies (Nadeem and Metcalf, 2007). However, there were also indications that flexible working in itself could be a source of stress (Ashforth, Kreiner and Fugate, 2000; Kelliher and Anderson, 2008; Tietze and Musson, 2005). Where different types of flexible working arrangements were examined separately, remote working was found to be a source of stress, both as a result of role conflict and role overload. Working at home was sometimes observed to be a source of stress, due to role conflict experienced by trying to attend to demands from both work and home roles (Kraut, 1989; Moore, 2006). Studies also suggested that working remotely might result in lower levels of employee support in comparison to that available to those present at the workplace (Trent, Smith and Wood, 1994) and that remote workers might experience greater conflict with co-workers (Gajendran and Harrison, 2007). Still, some studies have found no difference in well-being between those who worked remotely and those who were based at the workplace (Staples, 2001; Trent et al., 1994). In addition, schedule flexibility was also found to be associated with lower levels of stress (Shinn, Wong, Simko and Ortiz-Torres, 1989; Sparks, Faragher and Cooper, 2001), especially where the organisational culture was supportive of this type of flexibility. Through increased employee control, it was found to decrease work-family conflict and have a positive effect on a range of mental and physical health outcomes (Costa, Akerstedt, Nachreiner, Baltieri, Carvalhais, Folkard, Dresen, Gadbois, Gartner, Sukalo, Härmä, Kandolin, Sartori and Silvério, 2004, 2006; Glass and Finley, 2002; Thomas and Ganster, 1995).

The association between flexible working and well-being has continued to attract research attention. Interestingly, perhaps as a reflection of the state of knowledge relating to the various types of flexible working arrangements and various aspects of well-being, several articles have attempted to appraise the accumulated evidence in relation to flexible working and employee well-being. Some literature reviews have examined well-being as part of general themes in the literature concerning flexible working (e.g. Bessa and Tomlinson, 2017), while others have specifically focussed on outcomes associated with particular types of flexible working arrangements (e.g. Allen et al., 2015). Recent meta-analyses have been concerned with specific outcomes, such as work-family conflict (e.g. Allen, Johnson, Kiburz and Shockley, 2013), as well as likely moderators of the associations identified.

Based on 43 studies reporting evidence on the relationship between two types of flexible working arrangements (flexitime and telecommuting) and employees' psychological health, a meta-analysis by Kröll et al. (2017) concluded that both types of flexible working arrangements were related to employee psychological health. In a review of the extant evidence specifically relating to teleworking, Allen et al. (2015) found that, although the effect was small, teleworking was associated with significantly lower work-role stress and work exhaustion and that these relationships were partially mediated by increased autonomy. Furthermore, their review found evidence that both extent and frequency of telecommuting were negatively related to work exhaustion. Looking specifically at the relationship between flexible working arrangements and work-family conflict, Allen et al. (2013) conducted a meta-analysis using 61 samples reported in 58 papers. Overall, they found that flexible working arrangements were negatively associated with work interference with family (WIF). When looking at types of flexible working arrangements separately, they found that flexibility over time had a stronger effect than flexibility over place on WIF and also that the use of flexible working arrangements had a stronger effect than their availability.

Anderson, Kaplan and Vega (2015) investigated the relationship between remote working and well-being, using a sample of workers from a large US federal agency, who on average teleworked for more than half of the working week and had been doing so for around three years. They found that employees reported more job-related positive affective well-being and less job-related negative affective well-being on days when they teleworked, compared to when they worked from the office. Furthermore, this relationship was moderated by several individual differences. The relationship between telework and positive affect was more strongly positive for individuals who were high in openness to experience, lower in trait rumination and with greater social connectedness. Ter Hoeven and van Zoonen (2015) examined what they termed flexible work designs, based on temporal and spatial flexibility and well-being, using the Mood and Anxiety Symptom Questionnaire (Wardenaar et al., 2010). They noted that such arrangements offered advantages but also challenges for employee well-being. Their study, drawing on responses from 999 Dutch employees, found that flexible working arrangements were associated with employee well-being, through better work–life balance, greater autonomy and more effective communications, but negatively associated with well-being through interruptions to work processes. Vahle-Hinz, Kirschner and Thomson (2013) argued that the employment relationship may be a further source of stress for flexible workers. Their study showed that job control buffers the health impact of employment related demands.

In an interview-based qualitative study, Galea, Houkes and De Rijk (2014) explored how the use of flexibility over working hours influenced respondents' work–life balance. Their study revealed that respondents placed high value on the use of flexibility over working hours to balance work with their non-work lives, and those who had significant family responsibilities considered it a necessity, rather than merely a benefit. Their findings also highlight the importance of management support and fit with the work culture in implementing this type of flexibility. Taking a different approach, Bryan and Sevilla (2017) examined the link between access to flexible working arrangements and couples' synchronisation of their work schedules, arguing that the ability of couples to spend time together is central to work–life balance. Using data from the British Household Panel Survey wave 13, they found that access to flexitime increased synchronisation of work schedules for couples and particularly for those with children and as result, they argued, contributed to a better work–life balance.

Several studies examined the link with role conflict, specifically in terms of work and family roles and the outcomes of such conflict. For example, De Sivatte and Guadamillas (2013) found that the availability of flexible working arrangements was associated with decreased work-to-family conflict (WFC). In addition, however, they found that employee perceptions of a favourable work-family culture were also negatively related to WFC and that this was stronger than that with the availability of flexible working arrangements. Masuda et al. (2012) investigated the associations of availability of flexible working arrangements with both time and strain-based work-to-family conflict, drawing on data from several countries. Grouping countries into clusters, they found that for managers in the Anglo cluster, only flexitime was negatively associated with both time- and strain-based WFC. For Latin American managers, working part-time was negatively related to strain-based WFC. And for Asian managers, whilst flexitime was unrelated to time-based WFC, telecommuting was positively associated with strain-based WFC. Focussing specifically on control over working time, Lyness et al. (2012) focussed on the relationship between schedule control and strain-based work-family conflict, using secondary data from the 1997 ISSP Work Orientations Survey from 21 countries. Interestingly, they showed that schedule control was not related to strain-based WFC for the total sample but, across all countries in the study, there was a significant relationship with strain-based WFC for women, for whom greater control led to reduced levels of WFC.

Overall, in spite of continued work in this area, the evidence in relation to stress and well-being is less consistent. This may in part be because different indicators have been used, but it also potentially implies a more complicated relationship. While some studies suggest that enhanced employee control is associated with less stress and better well-being, not all studies found evidence of an association.

Factors influencing the relationship between flexible working arrangements and outcomes

In our earlier review, we noted the absence of studies which investigated the factors influencing the relationship between use and availability of flexible working arrangements and various outcomes. As such, we called for future research to explore the moderators of this relationship, at both the individual and organisational levels. In the intervening period, how the relationship works in more depth and factors that affect the intensity of the relationship have been examined. Hence, in addition to those studies already reported above, next we will briefly consider a number of further studies. These include both quantitative analyses that have formally tested for moderators and studies that have drawn on qualitative data to investigate the way in which the relationship operates in depth. First, we will report on those that have examined the relationship of the availability and use flexible working arrangements and the outcomes reported previously (job satisfaction, organisational commitment and employee well-being) and closely associated outcomes. We will then briefly report on studies which examine the influences on other outcomes that we judge to be of relevance.

Influences on outcomes reported previously

Chen and Fulmer (2018) examined the relationship between the number of flexible working arrangements employees perceived to be available to them and both job satisfaction and organisational commitment as reported previously; however, they further examined whether this relationship was moderated by the actual reported number of formal policies offered by the organisation and any differences between different types of flexible working arrangements (schedule flexibility, flexibility over location, flexibility over number of hours worked). Their findings demonstrated that the strength of the positive association between flexible working and job satisfaction and organisational commitment was influenced by the number and type of flexible working arrangement offered. Using the same dataset and building on Hobfoll's (2001) work, Wood et al. (2018) argued that the use of work/non-work supports is likely to be an act of proactive coping, aimed particularly at enhancing some resources (e.g. job control), to prevent, or reduce the loss of time and energy resulting from the work/non-work interface.

Rudolph and Baltes (2017) sought to explore how access to and usage of flexible working influences levels of work engagement, drawing on the results of two studies. Their evidence suggests that having access to, greater and more frequent use of flexible working arrangements does not have the same effect on all respondents. Rather, their findings show that the influence of flexible working arrangements on work engagement is contingent upon age and health. Although overall older workers were more likely to be engaged, being able to access and use more flexible working arrangements brought younger, healthier workers to a level of engagement that was equivalent to that of older workers, irrespective of health status.

Related to organisational commitment, Choi (2018), as mentioned previously, examined the relationship between teleworking and turnover intention. Specifically, they tested the moderating role of institutional support (measured by the level of take-up, assuming that this reflected encouragement to use the programme and a culture of understanding and support for employees' needs) and managerial support for work–life balance and respect for employee needs, although not directly support for teleworking.

Their analysis revealed that both institutional and managerial support moderated the negative association between telework and turnover intention and that the combined effect of institutional and managerial support had the greatest effect on turnover intention, highlighting the importance of active support in retaining teleworkers. Furthermore, they found that employees who had more intensive interaction with their co-workers also reported lower turnover intentions.

Focussing on well-being outcomes, Biron and Van Veldhoven (2016) examined the relationship between where teleworkers worked (home or at the office) and both their ability to concentrate and their 'need for recovery' from work, defined as the individual's desire for temporary relief from stressors in order to recuperate and replenish resources. Further, they explored a three-way interaction between job demands, control over working time and control over work location on the ability to concentrate and the need for recovery. The findings showed that the ability to concentrate and the need for recovery was lower on days when teleworkers worked from home than in the office. However, analysing the moderating effect of control over working time, they found that the generally higher level of control over working time when at home increased the association between job demands and the need for recovery, but that this association was reversed when control over working time was moderate. In comparison, no differences were observed when teleworkers worked at the office. For ability to concentrate, although employees were more able to concentrate on days spent working from home, where job demands were high, no differences were observed in relation to control over working time.

Influences on other outcomes

Thompson, Payne and Taylor (2015) examined the relationship between flexible working and anticipated organisational support and organisational attraction, separating out flexibility over working time and flexibility over the physical location of work. Using an experimental approach where prospective employees rated hypothetical organisations offering flexibility over time and space, the results showed a positive association for both types of flexibility in relation to anticipated organisational support and organisational attraction. Their analysis of potential moderators found preference for integration (as opposed to separation) of work and non-work roles as significant, where individuals with a strong preference for integration were significantly more attracted to organisations that offered flexibility over time and place.

Teasdale (2013) considered the implications of flexible working for professional women in an environment based on male models of working, on their relationships with co-workers and how this was influenced by organisational and job-related factors and on the individual's life course stage. Based on exploratory interviews, the findings identify both resentment and support from co-workers. Support was found to stem from empathy, solidarity and awareness of legal entitlement, whereas the source of resentment was based in perceptions of fairness and the need for co-workers to facilitate flexible working by covering and taking on extra workload. In a slightly different vein, Koivisto and Rice (2016) examined the relationship between access to flexible working arrangements and employees feeling respected and their endorsement of leaders. They explored the moderating effect of leader's representativeness of group identity (prototypicality) on these relationships. Their findings showed that employees who had access to flexible working arrangements felt more respected and expressed stronger endorsement of their leaders. Both of these were moderated by the leaders' representatives of group identity, but in opposite ways. Respect increased slightly with higher prototypicality, but leader endorsement increased with lower prototypicality.

Crowley and Kolenikov (2014) attempted to go beyond the availability and use of flexible working arrangements by focussing on the employees' sense of control over the options available to them. In other words, their perception of the power they held to help them manage their work–life balance through the availability and use of these policies. Specifically, they examined how mothers' evaluation of their control over flexible working arrangements (scheduling of working hours, schedule predictability, number of hours worked and where they worked) and time-off options (short-term time off to address both predictable and unpredictable needs, episodic time off for regular occurring activities and extended time off) influenced their perceptions of how their parenting responsibilities harmed their careers in relation to earnings, pay raises/promotions and job evaluations. Using data from a random sample of mothers in the USA, they found that control over flexible working arrangements had no significant impact on perceptions of career outcomes. Since control over the timing and location of work did not affect their perceptions of how their employers had treated them, they argued that flexible working arrangements provide options on how work can be completed, but do not impact on the quantity or quality of work that need to be delivered. Alternatively, time-off options were found to reduce perceptions of career harm due to parenting responsibilities.

Also considering control, Donnelly (2006), based on a case study of a consulting firm, examined how the interdependent nature of the employment relationship for knowledge workers influenced the degree of autonomy open to them over where and when they worked. The findings showed that although their knowledge and skills constituted a core organisational asset and therefore shifted bargaining power in their favour, their autonomy was limited, particularly for more senior knowledge workers, due to the client-dependency of the firm and resulting need to respond to their expectations in relation to speed and quality of work delivered.

Several of the studies explored the role of gender. Greenberg and Landry (2011), concerned with exploring how flexible working arrangements are negotiated, examined how women's perceptions of power and organisational work–life support influenced negotiations for flexible working. Their findings showed that individuals' perceptions of their own power, and hence relative bargaining power, influenced the tone of the negotiations, as well as the outcomes. Cultural work–life support (the extent to which cultural norms and social interactions were seen as supportive of work–life issues) was found to influence negotiation behaviour and structural work–life support (the extent to which formal policies and practices were seen as supportive of employees work–life interests) was found to influence outcomes. An interaction effect was found between power and work–life support in that where structural work–life support existed, power had less of an influence on negotiated outcomes in comparison to where there was no structural work–life support. Also focussing on gender, Donnelly (2015) explored the organisation of careers and flexibility for male and female management consultants in the UK and USA. The findings illuminate the role of national and organisational level policies on flexible working and the nature of work, including the prominence of client focus, in gendering careers and flexible working. Drawing on interview data comparing national contexts, the existence of the 'right to request' flexible working legislation in the UK was seen to have a limited effect on availability, type or uptake of flexible working. The take-up of flexible working was largely by female employees, and although part-time was not prevalent, it was more common in the UK and amongst women, but became increasingly less common at higher levels in the organisational hierarchy. Part-time working was perceived to impact negatively on careers, since working part-time was seen as an impediment to meeting client expectations and occupational norms. Thus, those seeking flexibility (mostly women) were steered to other types of flexible working, tending to be seen as a means of helping employees cope with the demands of their work, rather than reducing their working hours.

Examining the influence on organisational performance, measured by profit and/or occupation, Tardivo and Bollani (2016) developed a theoretical statistical model demonstrating that for different performance criteria (economic, social), faced with fluctuations in demand for a product or service, the employer would optimise performance through a mix of standard full-time and flexible workers. Consequently, as most services are subject to varying intra-day demand, the argument of win-win scenarios where employer-employee needs are matched can be explored.

4   Observations and conclusions

Conceptual and methodological issues

In our previous review, we concluded that the majority of studies had not been explicitly designed to investigate how giving some degree of choice over working arrangements could impact performance. We observed that many analyses had focussed on cross-sectional data, where different types of flexible working arrangements had often been examined together with more general family- or carer-friendly policies. Studies that had examined specific types of flexible working had often not taken contingency factors into account, such as the extent of choice available to the employee, the degree of change to the working arrangement, how the arrangement had been established or how long flexible working had been in operation. There were also significant differences in measurements and sample sizes used which hindered direct comparisons being made between studies. Although a range of outcomes had been considered and there were more consistent findings with respect to employee outcomes, most of this evidence was based on relatively small samples or had been gathered in the context of a single organisation. Overall, we concluded that the large variance in the design of studies was a plausible explanation for the mixed findings we observed in the literature and, in turn, our inability to establish a business case for flexible working arrangements. We expressed concerns about the definitions and methodology used and argued that greater clarity in relation to these was needed in future studies. We observed a predominance of cross-sectional survey-based studies and reviews of the literature, and thus argued that future qualitative and multi-method studies could lead to greater theory building. We also noted that studies tended to focus on a single unit of analysis and neglected time as a dimension; hence we argued for the development of multi-level and longitudinal analyses.

Considering the literature that has been published since our previous review, a number of these concerns remain. As discussed earlier and as shown in Table 3.1, there is still wide variation over what is meant by flexible working and what is measured in different studies. The body of evidence on this topic may therefore be subject to the jingle-jangle fallacy, where several meanings are attributed to one construct label (jingle), or where different labels are used for one construct (jangle), resulting in incorrect assumptions that different things are the same because they have the same label, or that they are different because their labels differ (Kelley, 1927). There also remains a divide between studies that bundle different flexible working arrangements together for the purposes of analysis (most typically flexibility over time and place) and those that examine either a single type of flexible working arrangements, or analyse each type separately. These are largely based on different assumptions and draw on different theories, with those that bundle types together assuming that it is having choice over working arrangements that yield performance-related outcomes and those that examine them separately attributing specific outcomes to the nature of each type of arrangement.

Notwithstanding these observations, the literature has moved forward in a number of areas. There have been attempts to provide greater clarity in relation to research design and greater acknowledgement of limitations. This evolution can be observed particularly in the more recent meta-analyses, whose selection criteria are made explicit and as such imply that the conclusions drawn are based on significantly smaller subsets of studies. There have also been more refined approaches designed to disentangle aspects of flexible working, such as the study by Biron and Van Veldhoven (2016) which examined teleworkers responses on days that they teleworked and days they were in the office. Recent studies using structural equation models have strengthened our knowledge with respect to the likely mediators and moderators of various relationships. Whilst it is still the case that only a small number of studies examining flexible working arrangements actually address performance directly, further insights have been developed into behavioural, attitudinal and well-being outcomes, which may contribute indirectly to performance. Interestingly, there is now evidence that the ability to work flexibly can be a contingent factor in the link between human resource management practices and well-being. For example, having access to and using flexible working arrangements may moderate the association between work-family conflict and employee attitudes (e.g. Sok, Blomme and Tromp, 2014), since flexible working arrangements can increase the perception of control over how work is carried out, as theorised and tested by Wood et al. (2018). However, in a related study based on the same data, the idea that flexible working arrangements would make high-performance working environments more attractive to women was challenged, given that the extent of availability of flexible working did not moderate the link between high-performance work systems and retention (Stirpe and Zárraga-Oberty, 2017). There is therefore evidence that the role of flexible working arrangements can vary with the type of arrangement, and consequently there are opportunities for further theory development and, as is the case in other research fields, there may be need to revisit data and replicate past studies.

The recent growth in multi-level studies, taking advantage of the availability of cross-national surveys, has shown how cultural variables can influence perceptions and outcomes of flexible working arrangements (e.g. Masuda et al., 2012). In doing so, they also support arguments in the HRM literature concerning how employee perceptions of management practices may impact attitudes and well-being and, ultimately, employee performance. In this vein, our understanding of the potential mediators has improved, but mediation may also vary with context. While some have concluded that the ability to work flexibly was linked to lower levels of absences and labour turnover, Possenriede et al.'s (2016) study questioned indirect effects via job satisfaction on labour supply. Taken together, the more recent literature adds to our previous observations that findings do not corroborate across sources or methods.

On a positive note, the recent literature has included a range of different outcomes (women's career progression, gender pay differentials, voluntary work behaviours enabled by ICT, team collaboration) which provide a picture of how changes to work arrangements may impact individual, group and wider behaviour. For example, Goldin and Katz (2016) have argued that temporal flexibility is likely to explain the low gender wage gap found in the US pharmaceutical sector. Similarly, Chung and van der Horst (2018) noted that flexible working arrangements are often credited with helping women resume work after the birth of their first child, and therefore can help in enabling a greater number of women attain leadership positions. More recently, Schlachter, McDowall, Cropley and Inceoglu (2018) examined the link between temporal flexibility and remote working and the intensity of voluntary use of work-related ICT and highlighted the gaps in understanding this behaviour, particularly in relation to what is known as the empowerment-enslavement paradox. Their observations suggest that the intensity of voluntary use of work-related ICT is likely to impact outcomes of flexible working arrangements in a different way from those identified in Lehdonvirta's (2018) analysis of flexible workers in a platform or gig economy environment. The latter illustrated how different designs and supporting mechanisms in a platform could help flexible workers using the platform to cope with procrastination, isolation and the perceived stigma of working from home. Moreover, both studies considered what had been identified as flexibility stigma (Stone and Hernandez, 2013). Although this has often been seen as predominantly a problem for mothers, who by adopting flexible working arrangements were seen to deviate from the 'ideal worker' norm and as such were portrayed as less productive (O'Connor and Cech, 2018), they argue that in practice it is more widespread and varied. Furthermore, O'Connor and Cech (2018) showed that an individual's perception of flexibility bias can be linked to a reduction in their level of job satisfaction and engagement, and thus can impact their work–life balance independently of gender. Consequently, how line managers respond to flexible working arrangements can be important, as there is evidence that their exposure to them can lead to transformational and positive attitudes to flexible working arrangements (Sweet, Pitt-Catsouphes and James, 2017). How this in turn might dilute perceptions of bias, isolation or the need to demonstrate presence by means of extensive voluntary use of work-related ICT are issues worthy of further investigation.

In addition, different moderators have been explored, and there is some evidence in support of the role of line managers' perceptions in relation to the outcomes from flexible working, that gender and occupation may interact with different types of flexible working arrangements, and that both the local context and how flexible working arrangements are implemented can impact on outcomes. However, given that longitudinal studies remain rare in this field, how any effect may vary over time is a largely unexplored area, as is the analyses of potential spillover effects at different levels of analyses.

Future research agenda

Following our previous review of the literature, we identified a number of areas where further research was needed, as well as approaches that would enable a more nuanced and robust understanding of the relationship between flexible working arrangements and performance-related outcomes. First, we argued that studies were needed which were specifically designed to examine this relationship given different contexts, in order to allow the extent of real choice open to employees to be ascertained. Second, we proposed that more detail was required about the flexible working arrangements being examined (e.g. whether formal or informal, how long they had been in place, degree of change to working arrangement etc.) and also that greater attention needed to be paid to the definition and measure of performance used. We also argued the need for different types of studies to be conducted in order to allow for generalisations to be made, causality to be established and greater understanding of how the relationships worked, helping to build theory in this area.

Although, as we have discussed, the published research has progressed on a number of fronts, several of the ideas we identified for future research previously remain in need of further attention. Conceptual and definitional issues require refinement so that there is clarity in relation to what is being examined (e.g. use, availability, perceived availability; a single flexible working arrangement, more general choice over where and when work is carried out, together with other family/carer-friendly policies), in order to avoid the jingle-jangle fallacy observed in relation to work/non-work balance by Casper, Vaziri, Holliday Wayne and DeHauw (2018) as highlighted previously.

Further developments in relation to research design are also welcome, both to extend and enrich our understanding of the relationships that stem from different types of flexible working arrangements and to provide more robust empirical evidence. Studies which are based on large and diverse samples may allow scope for greater generalisations to be made. In particular, it would be helpful to include employees in different roles and in different industry contexts, thereby moving beyond the dominant focus in much work–life balance research on professional workers (Gattrell, Burnett, Cooper and Sparrow, 2013) and to include contemporary work contexts, such as platform work in the gig economy, where employees have multiple jobs, or different employment relationships such as temporary or zero-hours contracts (Kelliher et al., 2018). It would also be helpful to recognise the primary tensions identified by Putnam et al. (2014) in the way in which flexible working arrangements are developed, enacted and experienced (variable versus fixed, supportive versus unsupportive climates, equitable versus inequitable implementation) and design studies accordingly. More longitudinal studies are needed to allow causal relationships to be examined. Studies involving data collected at different time points in the duration of the flexible working arrangement may also shed light on whether employee responses change as the arrangement becomes more embedded and this type of working more commonplace. We also call for more multi-level studies, and for studies that allow for comparisons at different levels in the organisation, and that the recent trend in addressing different national cultural contexts is extended to consider regional variations within and across nations.

As observed previously, since our call for greater investigation of moderators and mediators, several researchers have examined these; however, further work is needed to develop our understanding of how the relationships between flexible working arrangements and performance-related outcomes operate. Qualitative studies, especially those part of a mixed-methods approach, such as the work of Ross and Ali (2017) on ICT-enabled flexible workers, may tease out hypotheses on the mechanisms of how the relationships operate and the significance of context.

In our previous review, we suggested that the relationship between flexible working arrangements and performance-related outcomes could be examined in the context of the wider HRM and performance debate, by considering flexible working arrangements as HRM practices.[1] Whilst few papers to date have explicitly attempted to do this (an exception is the study by Bal and Lange (2015) which addresses 'flexibility HRM'), a number of analyses have focussed on manager's attitudes and enactment of these practices as well as on the work climate, which are elements in the chain linking HRM practices and performance (Purcell and Kinnie, 2007). We propose that different types of flexible working arrangements deserve more explicit attention in the context of this wider framework.

A further area of research worthy of attention and of particular importance in the context of a changing world of work is the extent to which employer and employee demands for flexibility can be matched. As discussed in the introductory chapter, in both the academic literature and in practice, separate debates have developed in relation to flexibility of and for employees. Flexibility of employees is often seen as an operations management concern, primarily designed to manage labour in more flexible ways (e.g. temporary and part-time contracts, multi-skilling/tasking) to increase efficiency by matching supply and demand for labour more closely and achieve greater organisational agility, allowing more rapid responses to changes in the environment. Flexibility for employees is concerned with helping employees achieve a more satisfactory relationship between their work and non-work lives (e.g. working from home, flexibility over working hours, reduced hours working), which may improve employee well-being, recruitment and retention and can be a means to increase workforce diversity. However, in practice some of these working arrangements can appear similar, implying that there may be possibilities to match employer and employee demands for flexibility. This would go beyond existing work on the 'dual agenda' (Bailyn, 2006) by specifically examining the potential to have matched employer-employee flexibility, rather than just wider benefits. Gaining greater efficiency and organisational agility, coupled with the longer-term benefits from increased organisational commitment and job satisfaction, could yield significant organisational benefits.

Conclusions

The relationship between flexible working arrangements and performance-related outcomes has continued to attract research attention since our earlier review. There have been new empirical studies using more rigorous approaches, exploring a wider range of outcomes and the factors influencing the relationships. There have also been several attempts to appraise the extant evidence by conducting reviews and meta-analyses. Whilst there remain difficulties in making comparisons between studies, the more recent research is generally more supportive of the business and social benefits to be derived from enabling employees to have flexible working arrangements to assist them in achieving a better work–life balance. Nevertheless, the evidence appears to imply that benefits may vary with context and type of flexible working; thus in order to build a more robust support for these benefits and how sustainable they are, there is a need for further research designed to overcome the weaknesses observed here.

Note

1 We note, however, flexible working arrangement policies may differ from other HRM policies, in the sense that employees can opt to take advantage of them as opposed to being subject to them, as would be the case with, for example, a performance management policy.

References

Adams, R.J., Smart, P. and Huff, A.S. (2017). Shades of grey: Guidelines for working with the grey literature in systematic reviews for management and organizational studies. *International Journal of Management Reviews*, 19 (4), 432–454.

Agile Futures Forum (2013). *Understanding the Economic Benefits of Workforce Agility*. Agile Future Forum.

Alis, D., Karsten, L. and Leopold, J. (2006). From gods to godesses. *Time and Society*, 15 (1), 81–104.

Allen, T. (2001). Family-supportive work environments: The role of organizational perceptions. *Journal of Vocational Behavior*, 58, 414–435.

Allen, T.D., Golden, T.D. and Shockley, K.M. (2015). How effective is telecommuting? Assessing the status of our scientific findings. *Psychological Science in the Public Interest*, 16 (2), 40–68.

Allen, T.D., Johnson, R.C., Kiburz, K.M. and Shockley, K.M. (2013). Work-family conflict and flexible work arrangements: Deconstructing flexibility. *Personnel Psychology*, 66 (2), 345–376.

Almer, E.D. and Kaplan, S.E. (2002). The effects of flexible work arrangements on stressors, burnout, and behavioral job outcomes in public accounting. *Behavioral Research in Accounting*, 14 (1), 1–34.

Anderson, A.J., Kaplan, S.A. and Vega, R.P. (2015). The impact of telework on emotional experience: When, and for whom, does telework improve daily affective well-being? *European Journal of Work and Organizational Psychology*, 24 (6), 882–897.

Ashforth, B.E., Kreiner, G.E. and Fugate, M. (2000). All in a day's work: Boundaries and micro role transitions. *Academy of Management Review*, 25 (3), 472–491.

Atkinson, C. and Hall, L. (2009). The role of gender in varying forms of flexible working. *Gender, Work & Organization*, 16 (6), 650–666.

Atkinson, J. (1985). Flexibility: Planning for an uncertain future. *Manpower Policy and Practice*, 1, 26–29.

Bailey, D. and Kurland, N. (2002). A review of telework research: Findings, new directions and lessons for the study of modern work. *Journal of Organisational Behaviour*, 23, 383–400.

Bailyn, L. (2006). *Breaking the Mould: Redesigning Work for Productive and Satisfying Lives*. Ithaca, NY: Cornell University Press.

Bailyn, L., Fletcher, J.K. and Kolb, D. (1997). Unexpected connections: Considering employees' personal lives can revitalize your business. *Sloan Management Review*, 38 (4), 11–19.

Baird, M. and Williamson, S. (2009). Women, work and Industrial Relations in 2008. *Journal of Industrial Relations*, 51 (3), 331–346.

Bal, P.M. and De Lange, A.H. (2015). From flexibility human resource management to employee engagement and perceived job performance across the lifespan: A multi sample study. *Journal of Occupational & Organizational Psychology*, 88 (1), 126–154.

Bal, P.M. and Dorenbosch, L. (2015). Age-related differences in the relations between individualised HRM and organisational performance: a large-scale employer survey. *Human Resource Management Journal*, 25 (1), 41–61.

Bal, P.M. Kleef, M. and Jansen, P.G.W. (2015). The impact of career customization on work outcomes: boundary conditions of manager support and employee age. *Journal of Organizational Behavior*, 36 (3), 421–440.

Baltes, B., Briggs, T., Huff, J., Wright, J. and Neuman, G. (1999). Flexible and compressed workweek schedules: A meta-analysis of their effects on work-related criteria. *Journal of Applied Psychology*, 84, 496–513.

Barley, S.R., Meyerson, D.E. and Grodal, S. (2011). E-mail as a source and symbol of stress. *Organization Science*, 22 (4), 887–906.

Batt, R. and Valcour, M. (2003). Human resource practices as predictors of work-family outcomes and employee turnover. *Industrial Relations*, 42, 189–220.

Beatson, M. (1995). *Labour Market Flexibility*. Employment Department Research Series. London.

Bergstrom, O. and Storrie, D. (2003). *Contingent Employment in Europe and the United States*. Cheltenham, UK: Edward Elgar Publishing.

Berkery, E., Morley, M.J., Tiernan, S., Purtill, H. and Parry, E. (2017). On the uptake of flexible working arrangements and the association with human resource and organizational performance outcomes. *European Management Review*, 14 (2), 165–183.

Bessa, I. and Tomlinson, J. (2017). Established, accelerated and emergent themes in flexible work research. *Journal of Industrial Relations*, 59 (2), 153–169.

Biron, M. and van Veldhoven, M. (2016). When control becomes a liability rather than an asset: Comparing home and office days among part-time teleworkers. *Journal of Organizational Behavior*, 37 (8), 1317–1337.

Branine, M. (2003). Part-time work and job sharing in Health Care: is the NHS a family-friendly employer? *Journal of Health and Organization and Management*, 17, 53–68.

Brough, P., O'Driscoll, M. and Kalliath, T. (2005). The ability of family-friendly organizational resources to predict work-family conflict and job and family satisfaction. *Stress and Health*, 21, 223–234.

Bryan, M.L. and Sevilla, A. (2017). Flexible working in the UK and its impact on couples' time coordination. *Review of Economics of the Household*, 15 (4), 1415–1437.

Bryson, C. (1999). Managing uncertainty or managing uncertainly? In: J. Leopold, L. Harris and T. Watson (eds.), *Strategic Human Resourcing*. London: Financial Times/Pitman Publishing, 63–88.

Butts, M.M., Caspar, W. and Yang, T.S. (2012). How important are work-family support policies? A meta analytic investigation of their effects on employee outcomes. *Journal of Applied Psychology*, 98, 1–25.

Butts, M.M., Casper, W.J. and Yang, T.S. (2013). How important are work – Family support policies? A meta-analytic investigation of their effects on employee outcomes. *Journal of Applied Psychology*, 98 (1), 1–25.

Cammann, C., Fichman, M., Jenkins, D. and Klesh, J. (1979). *The Michigan Organizational Assessment Questionnaire.* Unpublished manuscript. Ann Arbor, MI: University of Michigan.

Campbell-Clark, S. (2001). Work cultures and work-family balance. *Journal of Vocational Behaviour*, 58, 348–365.

Casey, B., Keep, E. and Mayhew, K. (1999). Flexibility, quality and competitiveness. *National Institute Economic Review*, 168, 70–81.

Casper, W.J., Eby, L.T., Bordeaux, C. and Lockwood, A. (2007). A review of methods in IO/OB work-family research. *Journal of Applied Psychology*, 92 (1), 28–41.

Casper, W.J., Vaziri, H., Holliday Wayne, J. and DeHauw, S. (2018). The jingle-jangle of work-nonwork balance: A comprehensive and meta-analytic review of its meaning and measurement. *Journal of Applied Psychology*, 103 (2), 182–214.

Chen, Y. and Fulmer, I.S. (2018). Fine-tuning what we know about employees' experience with flexible work arrangements and their job attitudes. *Human Resource Management*, 57 (1), 381–395.

Choi, S. (2018). Managing flexible work arrangements in Government: Testing the effects of institutional and managerial support. *Public Personnel Management*, 47 (1), 26–50.

Chow, I.H. and Keng-Howe, I.C. (2006). The effect of alternative work schedules on employee performance. *International Journal of Employment Studies*, 14 (1), 105–131.

Christensen, K and Staines, G. (1990). Flexitime: a viable solution to work/family conflict. *Journal of Family Issues*, 11, 455–476.

Chung, H. (2018). 'Women's work penalty' in access to flexible working arrangements across Europe. *European Journal of Industrial Relations*, 25 (1), 23–40. doi:10.1177/0959680117752829

Chung, H. and van der Horst, M. (2018). Women's employment patterns after childbirth and the perceived access to and use of flexitime and teleworking. *Human Relations*, 71 (1), 47–72. doi:10.1177/0018726717713828

CIPD. (2014). *HR: Getting Smart About Agile Working*. Wimbledon: London: CIPD.

Clark, A.E. (2005). Your money or your life: Changing job quality in OECD countries. *British Journal of Industrial Relations*, 43 (3), 377–400.

Collins, P. and Kolb, D. (2012). Innovation in distributed teams: The duality of connectivity norms and human agency. In: C. Kelliher and J. Richardson (eds.), *New Ways of Organizing Work: Developments, Perspectives and Experiences*. New York: Routledge, 140–159.

Cooper, R. and Baird, M. (2015). Bringing the "right to request" flexible working arrangements to life: from policies to practices. *Employee Relations*, 37 (5), 568–581.

Costa, G., Akerstedt, T., Nachreiner, F., Baltieri, F., Carvalhais, J., Folkard, S., Dresen, M.F., Gadbois, C., Gartner, J., Sukalo, H.G., Härmä, M., Kandolin, I., Sartori, S. and Silvério, J. (2004). Flexible working hours, health, and well-being in Europe: Some considerations from a SALTSA project. *Chronobiology International*, 21 (6), 831–844.

Costa, G., Sartori, S. and Akerstedt, T. (2006). Influence of flexibility and variability of working hours on health and well-being. *Chronobiology International*, 23 (6), 1125–1137.

Council of Economic Advisers (2014). *Work–Life Balance and the Economics of Workplace Flexibility*. Retrieved 11 December 2018, from https://obamawhitehouse. archives.gov/files/documents/100331-cea-economics-workplace-flexibility.pdf

Cranfield School of Management (2008). *Flexible Working and Performance: Summary of Research*. London: Working Families.

Crowley, J.E. and Kolenikov, S. (2014). Flexible work options and mothers' perceptions of career harm. *The Sociological Quarterly*, 55 (1), 168–195.

Dalton, D.R. and Mesch, D.J. (1990). The impact of flexible scheduling on employee attendance and turnover. *Administrative Science Quarterly*, 35 (2), 370–387.

De Menezes, L.M. and Kelliher, C. (2011). Flexible working and performance: A systematic review of the evidence for a business case. *International Journal of Management Reviews*, 13 (4), 452–474.

De Menezes, L.M. and Kelliher, C. (2017). Flexible working, individual performance, and employee attitudes: Comparing formal and informal arrangements. *Human Resource Management*, 56 (6), 1051–1070.

De Menezes, L.M. and Wood, S. (2006). The reality of flexible working systems in Britain. *International Journal of Human Resource Management*, 17 (1), 106–138.

de Sivatte, I. and Guadamillas, F. (2013). Antecedents and outcomes of implementing flexibility policies in organizations. *The International Journal of Human Resource Management*, 24 (7), 1327–1345.

Dex, S. and Forth, J. (2009). Equality and diversity at work. In: K. Brown, W., Bryson, A. Forth and J. Whitfield (eds.), *The Evolution of the Modern Workplace*. Cambridge, UK: Cambridge University Press.

Dex, S. and Scheibl, F. (1999). Business performance and family-friendly policies. *Journal of General Management*, 24, 22–37.

Di Martino, V. and Wirth, L. (1990). Telework: A new way of working and living. *International Labour Review*, 129 (5), 529–554.

Donnelly, N., Proctor-Thomson, S.B. and Plimmer, G. (2012). The role of 'voice' in matters of 'choice': Flexible work outcomes for women in the New Zealand public services. *Journal of Industrial Relations*, 54 (2), 182–203.

Donnelly, R. (2006). How 'free' is the free worker? An investigation into the working arrangements available to knowledge workers. *Personnel Review*, 35 (1), 78–97.

Donnelly, R. (2015). Gender, careers and flexibility in consultancies in the UK and the USA: A multi-level relational analysis. *The International Journal of Human Resource Management*, 26 (1), 80–99.

DTI (1998). *Fairness at Work*. Cm 3968. London: Department of Trade and Industry.

Dunham, R.B., Pierce, J.L. and Castañeda, M.B. (1987). Alternative work schedules: Two field quasi-experiments. *Personnel Psychology*, 40 (2), 215–242.

Eaton, S.C. (2003). If you can use them: Flexibility policies, organizational commitment, and perceived performance. *Industrial Relations*, 42 (2), 145–167.

Edwards, C. and Robinson, O. (2004). Evaluating the business case for part-time working amongst qualified workers. *British Journal of Industrial Relations*, 42 (1), 167–183.

Equality and Human Rights Commission (2017). *Shake Up of Working Culture and Practices Recommended to Reduce Pay Gaps*. Retrieved from www.equalityhumanrights.com/en/our-work/news/shake-working-culture-and-practices-recommended-reduce-pay-gaps.

Eurofound (2010). *Eurofound Yearbook 2010*. Luxembourg: Publications Office of the European Communities.

Eurofound (2012). *Fifth European Working Conditions Survey*. Luxembourg: Publications Office of the European Union.

Eurofound (2013). *EU Employers Take Family-Friendly Working Seriously*. Retrieved 1 November 2018 from www.eurofound.europa.eu/sites/default/files/ef_files/ewco/surveyreports/EU1302011D/EU1302011D.pdf

Eurofound (2014). *Working Conditions and Job Quality: Comparing Sectors in Europe Overview Report*. Dublin.

Eurofound (2015). *Third European Company Survey – Overview Report: Workplace Practices – Patterns, Performance and Well-Being*. Luxembourg: Publications Office of the European Union.

Eurofound (2018). *Living and Working in Europe 2017*. Luxembourg: Publications Office of the European Union.

Eurofound and ILO (2017). *Working Anytime, Anywhere: The Effects on the World of Work*. Luxembourg: Publications Office of the European Union; Geneva: International Labour Office.

European Commission (2010). *Industrial Relations in Europe 2010*. Industrial Relations.

European Commission (2017). *Work–life Balance for Parents and Carers*. Procedure 2017/0085 (COD).

Facer, I. and Wadsworth, L. (2008). Alternative work schedules and work-family balance: a research note. *Review of Public Personnel Administration*, 28, 166–177.

Forsyth, S. and Polzer-Debruyne, A. (2007). The organisational pay-offs for perceived work–life balance support. *Asia Pacific Journal of Human Resources*, 45, 113–123.

Foster Thompson, L. and Aspinwall, K.R. (2009). The recruitment value of work/life benefits. *Personnel Review*, 38 (2), 195–210.

Frank, K.E. and Lowe, D.J. (2003). An examination of alternative work arrangements in private accounting practice. *Accounting Horizons*, 17, 139–151.

Gajendran, R.S. and Harrison, D.A. (2007). The good, the bad, and the unknown about telecommuting: Meta-analysis of psychological mediators and individual consequences. *The Journal of Applied Psychology*, 92 (6), 1524–1541.

Galea, C., Houkes, I. and De Rijk, A. (2014). An insider's point of view: How a system of flexible working hours helps employees to strike a proper balance between work and personal life. *The International Journal of Human Resource Management*, 25 (8), 1090–1111.

Galinsky, E., Matos, K. and Sakai-O'Neill, K. (2013). Workplace flexibility: A model of change. *Community, Work & Family*, 16 (3), 285–306.

Gattrell, C.J., Burnett, S.B., Cooper, C.L. and Sparrow, P. (2013). Work–life balance and parenthood: A comparative review of definitions, equity and enrichment. *International Journal of Management Reviews*, 15 (3), 300–316.

Glass, J.L. and Finley, A. (2002). Coverage and effectiveness of family-responsive workplace policies. *Human Resource Management Review*, 12 (3), 313–337.

Godart, O.N., Görg, H. and Hanley, A. (2017). Trust-based work time and innovation: Evidence from firm-level data. *ILR Review*, 70 (4), 894–918.

Golden, L. (2008). Limited access: Disparities in flexible work schedules and work-at-home. *Journal of Family and Economic Issues*, 29 (1), 86–109.

Goldin, C. and Katz, L.F. (2016). A most egalitarian profession: Pharmacy and the evolution of a family-friendly occupation. *Journal of Labor Economics*, 34 (3), 705–746.

Golembiewski, R.T., Hilles, R. and Kagno, M.S. (1974). A longitudinal study of flexi-time effects: Some consequences of an OD structural intervention. *The Journal of Applied Behavioral Science*, 10 (4), 503–532.

Golembiewski, R.T. and Proehl, C. (1978). A survey of the empirical literature on flexible work hours: Character and consequences of a major innovation. *Academy of Management Review*, 3, 837–853.

Greenberg, D. and Landry, E.M. (2011). Negotiating a flexible work arrangement: How women navigate the influence of power and organizational context. *Journal of Organizational Behavior*, 32 (8), 1163–1188.

Greene, C.N. (1984). Effects of alternative work schedules: A field experiment. *Academy of Management Proceedings*, 8 (1), 269–273.

Gregory, A. and Milner, S. (2009). Editorial: Work–life balance: A matter of choice? *Gender, Work & Organization*, 16 (1), 1–13.

Grover, S. and Crocker, K. (1995). Who appreciates family-responsive human resource policies: the impact of family-friendly policies on organizational attachment of parents and non-parents. *Personnel Psychology*, 48, 271–288.

Halpern, D.F. (2005). How time-flexible work policies can reduce stress, improve health, and save money. *Stress and Health*, 21 (3), 157–168.

Hammer, L.B., Kossek, E.E., Yragui, N.L., Bodner, T.E. and Hanson, G.C. (2009). Development and validation of a multidimensional measure of family supportive supervisor behaviours (FSSB). *Journal of Management*, 35 (4), 837–856.

Hannah, R. (1994). The trade-off between worker mobility and employer flexibility: recent evidence and implication. *Employee Benefits Journal*, 19, 23–25.

Harrick, E., Vanek, G. and Michlitsch, J. (1986). Alternate work schedules, productivity, leave usage and employee attitudes: A field study. *Public Personnel Management*, 15, 159–207.

Harvey, B. and Luthans, F. (1979). Flexitime: An empirical analysis of its real meaning and impact. *MSU Business Topics*, 27, 31–36.

Healy, G. (2004). Work–life balance and family friendly policies – in whose interest? *Work, Employment and Society*, 18 (1), 219–223.

Henly, J.R. and Lambert, S. (2009). *Precarious Work Schedules in Low Level Jobs: Implications for Work–life Interferences and Stress*. Paper presented at the

International Centre for Work and Family Conference, IESE Business School, Barcelona, Spain, 6–8 July.

Hill, E.J., Ferris, M. and Martinson, V. (2003). Does it matter where you work? A comparison of how three work venues influence aspects of work and personal/ family life. *Journal of Vocational Behavior*, 63 (2), 220–241.

Hill, E.J., Miller, B., Weiner, S. and Colihan, J. (1998). Influences of the virtual office on aspects of work and work/life balance. *Personnel Psychology*, 51, 667–683.

Hill, E., Mead, N., Dean, L., Hafen, D., Gadd, R., Palmer, A. and Ferris, M. (2006). Researching the 60-hour dual-earner workweek: an alternative to the 'opt-out revolution'. *American Behavioral Scientist*, 49, 1184–1203.

Hobfoll, S.E. (2001). The influence of culture, community, and the nested-self in the stress process: Advancing conservation of resources theory. *Applied Psychology: An International Review*, 50, 337–421.

Hofstede, G. (2001). *Culture's Consequences* (2nd edn.). Thousand Oaks, CA: Sage.

Hohl, K. (1996). The effects of flexible working arrangements. *Nonprofit Management and Leadership*, 7 (1), 69–86.

Hooker, H., Neathey, F., Casebourne, J. and Munro, M. (2007). *The Third Work–Life Balance Employee Survey: Main Findings*. Brighton: Institute for Employment Studies.

Hyland, M.M., Rowsome, C. and Rowsome, E. (2005). The integrative effects of flexible work arrangements and preferences for segmenting or integrating work and home roles. *Journal of Behavioral & Applied Management*, 6 (2), 141–160.

Johnson, E.N., Lowe, D.J. and Reckers, P.M.J. (2008). Alternative work arrangements and perceived career success: current evidence from the big four firms in the US. *Accounts, Organizations and Society*, 33, 48–72.

Kalleberg, A.L. (2003). Flexible firm and labor market segmentation. *Work and Occupations*, 30 (2), 154–175.

Kauffeld, S., Jonas, E., and Frey, D. (2004). Effects of a flexible work-time design on employee and company related aims. *European Journal of Work and Organizational Psychology*, 13, 79–100.

Keizer, A. (2013). *Unions and their Representation of Contingent Workers: A Comparative Analysis of Japan, the Netherlands and the UK*. 10th European ILERA Conference, Amsterdam, 20–22 June.

Kelley, T.L. (1927). *Interpretation of Educational Measurements*. New York, NY: World Book.

Kelliher, C. and Anderson, D. (2008). For better or for worse? An analysis of how flexible working practices influence employees' perceptions of job quality. *International Journal of Human Resource Management*, 19 (3), 421–433.

Kelliher, C. and Anderson, D. (2010). Doing more with less? Flexible working practices and the intensification of work. *Human Relations*, 63 (1), 83–106.

Kelliher, C. and Gore, J. (2006). Functional flexibility and the intensification of work: transformation within service industries. In: P. Askenazy, D. Cartron, F. de Connick and M. Gollac (eds.), *Organisation et Intensite du Travail*. Toulouse: Octares, 93–102.

Kelliher, C., Gore, J. and Riley, M. (2002). *Re-Framing Functional Flexibility*. 20th Annual International Labour Process Conference, University of Strathclyde.

Kelliher, C. and Richardson, J. (2012). Recent developments in new ways of working. In: C. Kelliher and J. Richardson (eds.), *New Ways of Organizing Work: Developments, Perspectives and Experiences*. New York: Routledge, 1–15.

Kelliher, C., Richardson, J. and Boiarintseva, G. (2018). All of work? All of life? Reconceptualising work–life balance for the 21st century. *Human Resource Management Journal*. https://doi.org/10.1111/1748-8583.12215.

Kelliher, C. and Riley, M. (2003). Beyond efficiency: Some by-products of functional flexibility. *Service Industries Journal*, 23 (4), 98–113.

Kelly, E.L. and Kalev, A. (2006). Managing flexible work arrangements in US organizations: Formalized discretion or 'a right to ask'. *Socio-Economic Review*, 4 (3), 379–416.

Kelly, E. and Moen, P. (2007). Rethinking the clock of work: why schedule control may pay off at work and at home. *Advances in Developing Human Resources*, 9, 487–506.

Kelly, E., Kossek, E., Hammer, L., Durham, M., Bray, J., Chermack, K., Murphy, I. and Kaskubar, D. (2008). Getting there from here: research on the effects of work-family initiatives on work-family conflict and business outcomes. *Academy of Management Annals*, 2, 305–349.

Kim, J.S. and Campagna, A.F. (1981). Effects of flexitime on employee attendance and performance: A field experiment. *Academy of Management Journal*, 24 (4), 729–741.

Koivisto, S. and Rice, R.E. (2016). Leader prototypicality moderates the relation between access to flexible work options and employee feelings of respect and leader endorsement. *The International Journal of Human Resource Management*, 27 (22), 2771–2789.

Kopleman, R. (1985). Alternative work schedules and productivity: A review of the evidence. *National Productivity Review*, Spring, 150–165.

Kossek, E.E. and Lautsch, B.A. (2018). Work–life flexibility for whom? Occupational status and work–life inequality in upper, middle, and lower level jobs. *Academy of Management Annals*, 12 (1), 5–36.

Kossek, E.E., Lautsch, B.A. and Eaton, S.C. (2005). Flexibility enactment theory: Implications of flexibility type, control and boundary management for work-family effectiveness. In: E.E. Kossek and S.J. Lambert (eds.), *Work and Life Integration: Organisational, Cultural and Individual Perspectives*. Mahwah, NJ: Lawrence Erlbaum Associates, 243–261.

Kossek, E.E. and Lee, M.D. (2008). Implementing a reduced-workload arrangement to retain high talent: A case study. *The Psychologist-Manager Journal*, 11 (1), 49–64.

Kossek, E.E. and Ollier-Malaterre, A. (2012). Work–life policies: Linking national contexts, organizational practice and people for multi-level change. In: S. Poelmans, J.H. Greenhaus, and M. Las Heras Maestro. *Expanding the Boundaries of Work-Family Research. A Vision for the Future*. Basingstoke: Palgrave MacMillan.

Kossek, E.E., Ollier-Malaterre, A., Lee, M., Hall, T. and Pichler, S. (2011). *Managerial Gatekeeping Rationales for Customized Work Arrangements: Evidence of the Changing Employee-Organization Relationship*. Paper presented at SIOP, Chicago, IL.

Kossek, E.E. and Ozeki, C. (1999). Bridging the work-family policy and productivity gap: A literature review. *Community, Work and Family*, 2, 7–32.

Krausz, M. and Freibach, N. (1983). Effects of flexible working time for employed women upon satisfaction, strains, and absenteeism. *Journal of Occupational Psychology*, 56, 155–159.

Kraut, R.E. (1989). Telecommuting: The trade-offs of home work. *Journal of Communication*, 39 (3), 19–47.

Kröll, C., Doebler, P. and Nüesch, S. (2017). Meta-analytic evidence of the effectiveness of stress management at work. *European Journal of Work and Organizational Psychology*, 26 (5), 677–693.

Kurkland, N.B. and Bailey, D.E. (1999). The advantages and challenges of working here, there anywhere, and anytime. *Organizational Dynamics*, 28 (2), 53–68.

Lambert, S.J. and Waxman, E. (2005). Organization stratification: Distributing opportunities for balancing work and personal life. In: E.E. Kossek and S.J. Lambert (eds.), *Work and Life Integration: Organizational, Cultural, and Individual Perspectives*. Mahwah, NJ: Lawrence Erlbaum Associates, 103–126.

Lapierre, L. and Allen, T. (2006). Work-supportive family, family-supportive supervision, use of organizational benefits and problem-focused coping: implications for work-family conflict and employee well-being. *Journal of Occupational Health Psychology*, 11, 169–181.

Latack, J. and Foster, L. (1985). Implementation of compressed work schedules: participation and job redesign as critical factors for employee acceptance. *Personnel Psychology*, 38, 75–92.

Lautsch, B.A., Kossek, E.E. and Eaton, S.C. (2009). Supervisory approaches and paradoxes in managing telecommuting implementation. *Human Relations*, 62 (6), 795–827.

Lehdonvirta, V. (2018). Flexibility in the gig economy: Managing time on three online piecework platforms. *New Technology, Work and Employment*, 33 (1), 13–29.

Lewis, S. and den Dulk, L. (2010). Parents' experiences of flexible work arrangements in changing European workplaces. In: K. Christensen and B. Schneider (eds.), *Workplace Flexibility – Realigning 20th Century Jobs for a 21st Century Workforce*. Ithaca, NY: Cornell University Press.

Lewis, S., Gambles, R. and Rapoport, R. (2007). The constraints of a 'work–life balance' approach: An international perspective. *International Journal of Human Resource Management*, 18 (3), 360–373.

Lewis, S., Smithson, J., Cooper, C. and Dyer, J. (2001). *Flexible Futures: Flexible Working and Work–Life Integration: Summary of Findings From Stage 2*. Retrieved from www.workliferesearch.org.

Loretto, W. and Vickerstaff, S. (2015). Gender, age and flexible working in later life. *Work, Employment and Society*, 29 (2), 233–249.

Loretto, W., Vickerstaff, S. and White, P. (2005). *Older Workers and Options for Flexible Work*. Working Paper Series No. 31. Manchester. Equal Opportunities Commission.

Lott, Y. and Chung, H. (2016). Gender discrepancies in the outcomes of schedule control on overtime hours and income in Germany. *European Sociological Review*, 32 (6), 752–765.

Lyness, K.S., Gornick, J.C., Stone, P. and Grotto, A.R. (2012). It's All about Control. Worker control over schedule and hours in cross-national context. *American Sociological Review*, 77 (6), 1023–1049.

Madsen, S. (2003). The effects of home-based teleworking on work-family conflict. *Human Resource Development Quarterly*, 14, 35–58

Martin, B. and MacDonnell, R. (2012). Is telework effective for organizations?: A meta analysis of empirical research on perceptions of telework and organizational outcomes. *Management Research Review*, 35 (7), 602–616.

Martinez-Sanchez, A., Perez-Perez, M., Luis-Carnicer, P. and Vela-Jimenez, M. (2007a). Telework, human resource flexibility and firm performance. *New Technology, Work and Performance*, 22, 208–223.

Martinez-Sanchez, A., Perez-Perez, M., Luis-Carnicer, P. and Vela-Jimenez, M. (2007b). Teleworking and workplace flexibility: a study of impact on firm performance. *Personnel Review*, 36, 42–64.

Masuda, A.D., Poelmans, S.A.Y., Allen, T.D., Spector, P.E., Lapierre, L.M., Cooper, C.L., Abarca, N., Brough, P., Ferreiro, P., Fraile, G., Lu, L., Lu, C.-Q., Siu, O.L., O'Driscoll, M.P., Simoni, A.S., Shima, S. and Moreno-Velazquez, I. (2012). Flexible work arrangements availability and their relationship with work-to-family conflict, job satisfaction, and turnover intentions: A comparison of three country clusters. *Applied Psychology*, 61 (1), 1–29. doi:10.1111/j.1464-0597.2011.00453.x

Matusik, S.F. and Mickel, A.E. (2011). Embracing or embattled by converged mobile devices? Users' experiences with a contemporary connectivity technology. *Human Relations*, 64 (8), 1001–1030.

McCampbell, A.S. (1996). Benefits achieved through alternative work schedules. *Human Resource Planning*, 19 (3), 30–37.

Meyer, C., Mukerjee, S. and Sestero, A. (2001). Work-family benefits: Which ones maximise profits? *Journal of Managerial Issues*, 13 (1), 28–44.

Moen, P., Kelly, E.L. and Hill, R. (2011). Does enhancing work-time control and flexibility reduce turnover? A naturally occurring experiment. *Social Problems*, 58 (1), 69–98.

Moore, J. (2006). Homeworking and work–life balance: Does it add to quality of life? *Revue Europeene de Psychologie Appliquee*, 56 (1), 5–13.

Nadeem, S. and Metcalf, H. (2007). *Work–Life Policies in Great Britain: What Works, Where and How?* London: Department for Business, Enterprise and Regulatory Reform.

Narayanan, V.K. and Nath, R. (1982). A field test of some attitudinal and behavioral consequences of flexitime. *Journal of Applied Psychology*, 67 (2), 214–218.

National Care Strategy (GBR DfEE 1998). *Meeting the Childcare Challenge: A Framework and Consultation Document*. Department of Education and Employment.

Nollen, S.D. (1979). Does flexitime improve productivity? *Harvard Business Review*, 57 (5), 12–22.

Nollen, S.D. (1981). The compressed workweek: Is it worth the effort? *Industrial Engineer*, 13, 58–64.

O'Connor, L. and Cech, E.A. (2018). Not just a mothers' problem: The consequences of perceived workplace flexibility bias for all workers, *Sociological Perspectives*, 61 (5), 808–829. https://doi.org/10.1177/0731121418768235

Orpen, C. (1981). Effect of flexible working hours on employee satisfaction and performance: A field experiment. *Journal of Applied Psychology*, 66, 113–115.

Ozbilgin, M.F., Beauregard, T.A., Tatli, A. and Bell, M.P. (2011). Work–life, diversity and intersectionality: A critical review and research agenda. *International Journal of Management Reviews*, 13 (2), 177–198.

Peretz, H., Fried, Y. and Levi, A. (2018). Flexible work arrangements, national culture, organisational characteristics, and organisational outcomes: A study across 21 countries. *Human Resource Management Journal*, 28 (1), 182–200.

Perlow, L.A. (2012). *Sleeping With Your Smartphone: How to Break the 24/7 Habit and Change the Way You Work*. Boston, MA: Harvard Business Review Press.

Perry-Smith, J. and Dumas, T. (2007). *Debunking the Ideal Worker Myth: Effects of Temporal Flexibility and Family Configuration on Engagement*. Paper presented at the Academy of Management Annual Meeting, Philadelphia, USA.

Peters, P., Den Dulk, L. and Van Der Lippe, T. (2009). The effects of time-spatial flexibility and new working conditions on employees' work–life balance: The Dutch case. *Community, Work and Family*, 12 (3), 279–298.

Piasna, A. (2018). Scheduled to work hard: the relationship between non-standard working hours and work intensity among European workers (2005–2015). *Human Resource Management Journal*, 28 (1), 167–181.

Pierce, J.L. and Newstrom, J.W. (1980). Toward a conceptual clarification of employee responses to flexible working hours: A work adjustment approach. *Journal of Management*, 6 (2), 117–134.

Pierce, J.L. and Newstrom, J.W. (1982). Employee responses to flexible work schedules: An inter-organization, inter-system comparison. *Journal of Management*, 8 (1), 9–25.

Pierce, J.L. and Newstrom, J.W. (1983). The design of flexible work schedules and employee responses: Relationships and process. *Journal of Occupational Behavior*, 4, 247–262.

Pitt-Catsouphes, M., James, J.B., McNamara, T. and Cahill, K. (2015). Relationships between managers who are innovators/early adopters of flexible work options and team performance. *Journal of Change Management*, 15 (3), 167–187.

Pollert, A. (1991). *The Orthodoxy of Flexibility: Farewell to Flexibility?* Oxford: Blackwell.

Possenriede, D., Hassink, W.H. and Plantenga, J. (2016). Does temporal and locational flexibility of work increase the supply of working hours? Evidence from the Netherlands. *IZA Journal of Labor Policy*, 5 (1), 1–34.

Purcell, J. and Kinnie, N. (2007). HRM and business performance. In P. Boxall, J. Purcell and R. Wright (eds.), *Oxford Handbook of Human Resource Management*. Oxford: Oxford University Press, 533–552.

Putnam, L.L., Myers, K.K. and Gailliard, B.M. (2014). Examining the tensions in workplace flexibility and exploring options for new directions. *Human Relations*, 67 (4), 413–440.

Rainey, G. and Wolf, L. (1981). Flex-time: Short-term benefits; long term...? *Public Administrative Review*, January/February, 52–63.

Rogier, S. and Pagett, M. (2004). The impact of utilising a flexible work schedule on the perceived career advancement potential of women. *Human Resource Development Quarterly*, 15, 89–106.

Ronen, S. (1984). *Alternative Work Schedules: Selecting, Implementing and Evaluating.* Homewood, IL: Dow Jones-Irwin.

Ronen, S. and Primps, S. (1980). The impact of flextime on performance and attitudes in 25 public agencies. *Public Personnel Management,* 9 (3), 201.

Rose, E. (2017). Workplace temporalities: a time-based critique of the flexible working provisions. *Industrial Law Journal,* 46 (2), 245–267.

Ross, P. and Ali, Y. (2017). Normative commitment in the ICT sector: Why professional commitment and flexible work practices matter. *International Journal of Employment Studies,* 25 (1), 44–62.

Rothausen, T. (1994). Job satisfaction and the parent worker: the role of flexibility and rewards. *Journal of Vocational Behaviour,* 44, 317–336.

Rothbard, N.P., Phillips, K.W. and Dumas, T.L. (2005). Managing multiple roles: Work-family policies and individuals? Desires for segmentation. *Organization Science,* 16 (3), 243–258.

Rubery, J., Keizer, A. and Grimshaw, D. (2016). Flexibility bites back: The multiple and hidden costs of flexible employment policies. *Human Resource Management Journal,* 26 (3), 235–251.

Rudolph, C.W. and Baltes, B.B. (2017). Age and health jointly moderate the influence of flexible work arrangements on work engagement: Evidence from two empirical studies. *Journal of Occupational Health Psychology,* 22 (1), 40–58.

Sungjoo, C. (2018). Managing flexible work arrangements in Government: testing the effects of institutional and managerial support. *Public Personnel Management,* 47 (1), 26–50.

Scandura, T. and Lankau, M. (1997). Relationships of gender, family responsibility and flexible work hours to organisational commitment and job satisfaction. *Journal of Organizational Behavior,* 18 (4), 377–391.

Schein, V.E., Maurer, E.H. and Novak, J.F. (1977). Impact of flexible working hours on productivity. *Journal of Applied Psychology,* 62 (4), 463–465.

Schlachter, S., McDowall, A., Cropley, M. and Inceoglu, I. (2018). Voluntary work-related technology use during non-work time: A narrative synthesis of empirical research and research agenda. *International Journal of Management Reviews,* 20 (4), 825–846.

Shamir, B. and Salomon, I. (1985). Work at home and the quality of working life. *Academy of Management Review,* 10, 455–464.

Shepard III, E., Clifton, T., and Kruse, D. (1996). Flexible working hours and productivity: some evidence from the pharmaceutical industry. *Industrial Relations,* 35, 123–139.

Shinn, M., Wong, N.W., Simko, P.A. and Ortiz-Torres, B. (1989). Promoting the well-being of working parents: Coping, social support, and flexible job schedules. *American Journal of Community Psychology,* 17 (1), 31–55.

Shockley, K. and Allen, T. (2007). When flexibility helps: another look at the availability of flexibility work arrangements and work-family conflict. *Journal of Vocational Behavior,* 71, 479–493.

SHRM (2017). *2017 Employee Benefits. Remaining Competitive in a Challenging Talent Marketplace.* Alexandria, VA: Society for Human Resource Management.

Skyrme, D. (1994). Flexible working: Building a responsive organisation. *Long Range Planning*, 27 (5), 98–110.

Sok, J., Blomme, R., & Tromp, D. (2014). Positive and negative spillover from work to home: the role of organizational culture and supportive arrangements. *British Journal of Management*, 25 (3), 456–472.

Sparks, K., Faragher, B. and Cooper, C.L. (2001). Well-being and occupational health in the 21st century workplace. *Journal of Occupational and Organizational Psychology*, 74 (4), 489–509.

Staples, D.S. (2001). A study of remote workers and their differences from non-remote workers. *Journal of Organizational and End User Computing*, 13 (2), 3–14.

Stavrou, E.T. (2005). Flexible work bundles and organizational competitiveness: A cross-national study of the European work context. *Journal of Organizational Behavior*, 26 (8), 923–947.

Stavrou, E.T., Parry, E. and Anderson, D. (2015). Nonstandard work arrangements and configurations of firm and societal systems. *The International Journal of Human Resource Management*, 26 (19), 2412–2433.

Stirpe, L. and Zárraga-Oberty, C. (2017). Are high-performance work systems always a valuable retention tool? The roles of workforce feminization and flexible work arrangements. *European Management Journal*, 35 (1), 128–136.

Stone, P. and Hernandez, L.A. (2013). The all-or-nothing workplace: Flexibility stigma and 'opting out' among professional-managerial women. *Journal of Social Issues*, 69 (2), 235–256. doi:10.1111/josi.12013

Sweet, S., Pitt-Catsouphes, M. and James, J.B. (2017). Manager attitudes concerning flexible work arrangements: fixed or changeable? *Community, Work & Family*, 20 (1), 50–71.

Tardivo, G. and Bollani, L. (2016). Statistical model to investigate the contributions under flexible work conditions for workers and business. *Journal of Financial Management and Analysis*, 29 (1), 27–37.

Teasdale, N. (2013). Fragmented sisters? The implications of flexible working policies for professional women's workplace relationships. *Gender, Work & Organization*, 20 (4), 397–412.

ter Hoeven, C.L. and van Zoonen, W. (2015). Flexible work designs and employee well-being: Examining the effects of resources and demands. *New Technology, Work and Employment*, 30 (3), 237–255.

Thomas, L.T. and Ganster, D.C. (1995). Impact of family-supportive work variables on work-family conflict and strain: A control perspective. *Journal of Applied Psychology*, 80 (1), 6–15.

Thompson, C. Beauvais, L. and Lyness, K. (1999). When work-family benefits are not enough: the influence of work-family culture on benefit utilization, family attachment and work-family conflict. *Journal of Vocational Behavior*, 54, 392–415.

Thompson, R.J., Payne, S.C. and Taylor, A.B. (2015). Applicant attraction to flexible work arrangements: Separating the influence of flextime and flexplace. *Journal of Occupational and Organizational Psychology*, 88 (4), 726–749.

Thorgeirsdottir, T. and Kelliher, C. (2017). Changing interfaces: The implications of flexible work arrangement use on team collaboration. *Academy of Management Annual Meeting Proceedings*, 2017 (1), 1.

Tietze, S. and Musson, G. (2005). Recasting the home-work relationship: A case of mutual adjustment? *Organization Studies*, 26 (9), 1331–1352.

Todd, P. and Binns, J. (2013). Work–life balance: Is it now a problem for management? *Gender, Work & Organization*, 20 (3), 219–231.

Townsend, K., McDonald, P. and Cathcart, A. (2017). Managing flexible work arrangements in small not-for-profit firms: the influence of organisational size, financial constraints and workforce characteristics. *International Journal of Human Resource Management*, 28 (14), 2085–2107.

Trent, J.T., Smith, A.L. and Wood, D.L. (1994). Telecommuting: Stress and social support. *Psychological reports*, 74 (3 Pt 2), 1312–1314.

Troup, C. and Rose, J. (2012). Telecommuting: Does working from home have positive or negative outcomes for all employees? *Community, Work and Family*, 15 (4), 472–486.

UNECE (2010). *Measuring Quality of Employment: Country Pilot Reports Prepared by UNECE Task Force*. United Nations, Geneva, pp. 4–5.

Vahle-Hinz, T. Kirschner, K. and Thomson, M. (2013). Employment-related demands and resources – New ways of researching stress in flexible work arrangements. *Management Revue*, 24 (3), 199–221.

Van Dyne, L., Kossek, E. and Lobel, S. (2007). Less need to be there: Cross-level effects of work practices that support work–life flexibility and enhance group processes and group-level OCB. *Human Relations*, 60 (8), 1123–1154.

Van Velzen, M. and Wilthagen, T. (2006). In search of a balance: Flexibility and security strategies in employment protection legislation, temporary work and part-time work. *Bulletin of Comparative Labour Relations*, 59, 153–182.

Vargas, O. (2016). Employee-friendly working time flexibility: Prevalence and policies. *Foundation Focus*, 19, 8–9.

Vega, A. and Gilbert, M. (1997). Longer days, shorter weeks: compressed work weeks in policing. *Public Personnel Management*, 26, 391–402.

Venne, R. (1997). The impact of the compressed workweek on absenteeism. *Relations Industrielles/Industrial Relations*, 52, 382–400.

Vickerstaff, S., Baldock, J.C., Cox, J. and Keen, L. (2004). *Happy Retirement? The Impact of Employers' Policies and Practice on the Process of Retirement*. Bristol: The Policy Press

Walqing European Policy Brief (2010). *Work and Life Quality in New and Growing Jobs*. November, pp. 4–5.

Wang, P. and Walumbwa, F.O. (2007). Family-friendly programs, organizational commitment, and work withdrawal: The moderating role of transformational leadership. *Personnel Psychology*, 60 (2), 397–427.

Wardenaar, K.J., van Veen, T., Giltay, E.J., de Beurs, E., Penninx, B.W.J.H. and Zitman, F.G. (2010). Development and validation of a 30-item short adaptation of the Mood and Anxiety Symptoms Questionnaire (MASQ). *Psychiatry Research*, 179 (1), 101–106.

Whyman, P.B. and Petrescu, A.I. (2014). Partnership, flexible workplace practices and the realisation of mutual gains: evidence from the British WERS 2004 dataset. *International Journal of Human Resource Management*, 25 (6), 829–851.

Wise, S. and Bond, S. (2003). Work–life policy: does it do exactly what it says on the tin? *Women in Management Review*, 18, 20–31.

Wood, S., Daniels, K. and Ogbonnaya, C. (2018). Use of work-nonwork supports and employee well-being: The mediating roles of job demands, job control supportive management and work-nonwork conflict. *International Journal of Human Resource Management*.

Wood, S. and De Menezes, L. (2007). Family-friendly, equal-opportunity and high-involvement management in Britain. In: P. Boxall, J. Purcell and P. Wright (eds.), *Oxford Handbook of Human Resource Management*. Oxford: Oxford University Press, 581–598.

Wood, S. J., De Menezes, L. M. and Lasaosa, A. (2003). Family-friendly management in Great Britain: testing various perspectives. *Industrial Relations*, 42, 221–250.

Wood, S., Van Veldhoven, M., Croon, M. and de Menezes, L.M. (2012). Enriched job design, high involvement management and organizational performance: The mediating roles of job satisfaction and well-being. *Human Relations*, 65, 419–445.

Zeytinoglu, I., Cooke, G. and Mann, S. (2009). Flexibility: Whose choice is it anyway? *Industrial Relations*, 64 (6), 555–574.

Index

Note: page numbers in *italic* indicate a figure and page numbers in **bold** indicate a table on the corresponding page.

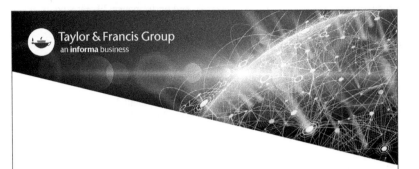